tech talk

Intermediate
Student's Book

Vicki Hollett • **John Sydes**

OXFORD
UNIVERSITY PRESS

CONTENTS

1 What's up?

Jobs

1 Have you ever taken an online training course? Would you like to take lessons via the internet instead of in a classroom? (Why / Why not?)

2 🎧 Some new employees are taking their company's online training course in corporate security. Listen and find out who they are and where they are. Complete the table.

Name	Where they work	Job	How long	Current projects
Larina Rios	—	1	—	—
George Paterson	2	3	4	5
April Wei	6	7	8 —	
Amar Kumar	9	10	11 —	
Joey Marino	—	12	13	14

3 🎧 Use the correct forms of verbs from the list to complete sentences from the conversation. Then listen again and check your answers.

> provide   work   get on   build   speak   settle in

1 I .... in the London Office.
2 We're .... a new warehouse.
3 We .... technical support.
4 We .... Korean, Japanese, and Mandarin.
5 How are you .... with your new job?
6 I'm .... to the office here very well.

Decide whether each statement is about temporary or long-term activities. What tenses did the speakers use?

Present tenses

Use the Present Simple to talk about long-term activities and things that are generally true.

+	?	–
*I **work** on the help desk.*	*What **do** you do?*	*We **don't** want to know.*
*He **works** in China.*	*What **does** it do?*	*It **doesn't** matter.*

Use the Present Continuous to talk about temporary activities that are in progress now.
+ *I'm **working** on a project.*   ? *Are you **settling in** OK?*   - *He **isn't telling** anyone.*

---

4 Complete some other introductions. Use the Present Simple or Continuous form of the verb in brackets.

1

Hi. I'm Sam Gonzales and I'm here to learn about your lighting products. I ....¹ (stay) for a week so I can meet all your designers and materials engineers. I ....² (work) for LBT & Hillard and we ....³ (design) shop interiors. So I ....⁴ (look for) new materials and technologies we can use to illuminate shops and stores more economically.

2

OK, well, I think most of you probably know me, but for those of you who don't, I'm Maria Mendos, and I ....¹ (run) a small company called Lab2, which ....² (make) miniature cameras for medical applications. We ....³ (produce) five models, and we currently ....⁴ (develop) two new models for endoscopies. My work ....⁵ (involve) a lot of market research as well as day-to-day administration. So at the moment I ....⁶ (travel) a lot to talk to doctors about a camera that can be used in heart surgery.

Present Perfect

The Present Perfect connects the past and the present.

I started working here yesterday.

PAST ↓ NOW

I've been here one day.
I've been working here for a day.
How long have you been working here?

5 Work with a partner. Ask and answer these questions.

1 What's your job?
2 How long have you been a(n) ....?
3 Where do you work / study?
4 How long have you been working / studying there?
5 Where do you live?
6 How long have you been living there?

6 Add the verb *do*, *are*, or *have* to make questions.

Example
   do
What/you do?
     /\\

1 What company you work for?
2 you been working there long?

3 you live in London?
4 Where you based?
5 How long you been based there?
6 you working on any interesting projects?
7 How you getting on?
8 What languages you speak?
9 How long you been learning English?
10 you taking any other training courses at the moment?

Practise asking and answering the questions with a partner.

7 Your company has sent you on a training course. It's the first day, and the trainer wants you to tell the class a little about yourself. Make some notes about these things, and plan what to say.

1 Company / Department
2 How long you've been working there
3 Job title
4 Anything you're in charge of or responsible for
5 Some things you do
6 A current project

8 Take turns to stand up and introduce yourself to the class. After each person has spoken, ask them two or three questions about their job, company, or current projects.

Emails

1 Read and match each email beginning to the best ending.

1

Hi Birgit,

Just a quick note to let you know I'll be in Portugal from tomorrow till Monday, 7 October.

2

Hi everyone,

Attached is a tentative schedule for the quality circle meeting. It hasn't been easy to fit so many presentations into the short time frame available, so could you make sure you start and finish promptly?

3

Dear Ms Olssen,

The new parts were shipped this morning and will arrive on Friday. We are very sorry that it has taken so long to straighten the problem out.

4

I'm writing regarding our phone call today about the 14 bearing housings that were not pre-drilled. We do not want replacements and we understand you will pay the shipment costs for their return.

5

Frank,

I've checked out flights and this one seems the best fit for your schedule:

6

Hi Marie,

Thanks for getting back to me so quickly about the mix up with the commas and decimal points in the specs.

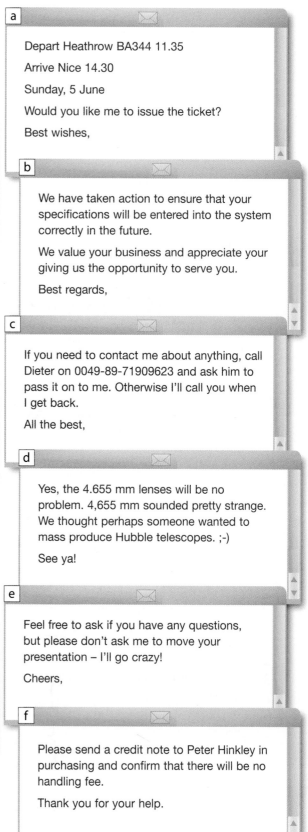

a

Depart Heathrow BA344 11.35

Arrive Nice 14.30

Sunday, 5 June

Would you like me to issue the ticket?

Best wishes,

b

We have taken action to ensure that your specifications will be entered into the system correctly in the future.

We value your business and appreciate your giving us the opportunity to serve you.

Best regards,

c

If you need to contact me about anything, call Dieter on 0049-89-71909623 and ask him to pass it on to me. Otherwise I'll call you when I get back.

All the best,

d

Yes, the 4.655 mm lenses will be no problem. 4,655 mm sounded pretty strange. We thought perhaps someone wanted to mass produce Hubble telescopes. ;-)

See ya!

e

Feel free to ask if you have any questions, but please don't ask me to move your presentation – I'll go crazy!

Cheers,

f

Please send a credit note to Peter Hinkley in purchasing and confirm that there will be no handling fee.

Thank you for your help.

2 Discuss these questions with a partner.

1 Which emails are more formal in tone and which are more informal?

2 What makes the emails more formal or informal? Can you find examples of words and phrases or other parts of the messages that are formal or informal?

3 When is it appropriate to address people with a title like Mr, Mrs, or Ms?

4 Is it ever OK to start an email without saying *Hi* or *Dear*?

5 Look at the last lines of the emails. Which endings are appropriate for:
  a professional contacts you don't know?
  b colleagues or friends you know well?
  c both?

6 What other expressions do people use to end emails? Which endings do you prefer?

3 A good subject line is brief and tells the reader what the email is about. Match this subject line to one of the emails on page 6.

Work with some other students and suggest subject lines for the other five emails.

4 Find and make a note of phrases in the emails that you can use to do these things.

Common email expressions	
Request action	*Could you...?*
Thank people for help	
Offer help	
Explain the reason(s) for the email	
Apologize	
Send an attachment	

Do the emails contain any other phrases you can use in the emails you write?

5 Read these situations. Suggest opening and closing lines for the emails you could send.

1 One of your clients wrote to you last week but you were away, so you're only just replying. They have lost some documentation on a piece of equipment. You can send it to them as an attachment.

2 You're the boss. Your team worked late last night to finish a project. You need them to work late again tonight to finish another important project. You would like to offer something as a token of your appreciation. Pizza perhaps, or maybe something else?

6 Work in pairs or groups. Choose one of the emails and write it together. One person writes, and the others check spelling and grammar.

7 Give your email to another pair or group and read theirs. Write a reply.

Specifications

1 Would you like to ride on a scooter like this? (Why / Why not?) Look at the information in the specifications. What could the specs be?

2 Here's the missing information. Write the items in the correct place in the spec list.

a Approximate shipping weight
b Maximum load
c Available colours
d Construction materials
e Diameter
f Engine
g Fuel
h Fuel tank capacity
i Approximate shipping packing size
j Height
k Maximum speed
l Operating time
m Price
n Delivery time
o Stopping distance

Compare your answers with another student. Then check them in file 6 on page 90.

3 What questions could you ask to get the information in the specifications?

Examples
How high is it? What's its height?
What's its diameter?

4 🎧 Listen to ten people asking some questions about the scooter. Find the answers to their questions in the spec list.

THE HOVER AIRBOARD SCOOTER

Looking more like a miniature flying saucer than a scooter, the Hover Airboard's engine-powered fan lifts you up and carries you along on a cushion of air.

SPECIFICATIONS

j	1	1200 mm including handle
e	2	1600 mm
k	3	25 km/h
o	4	6 m
b	5	100 kg
l	6	1 hour on a full tank of fuel
d	7	fibreglass / high-impact plastic shell / aluminium frame / rubber skirt
f	8	4-stroke Briggs & Stratton
h	9	5 L
g	10	85 octane unleaded
a	11	150 kg
i	12	800 mm H x 1800 mm W x 1800 mm L
c	13	red, blue, green, and yellow
n	14	8–10 weeks
m	15	$27,000

5 Complete the sentences with these words.

last   made of   cost   weight   take   kind of   come in   wide   heavy

Questions about specifications

We use many different questions to ask about specifications. Here are some important ones.

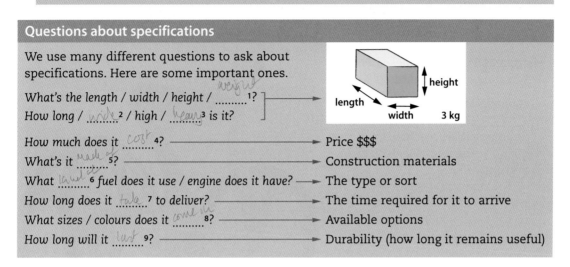

What's the length / width / height / ..weight..¹?
How long / ..wide..² / high / ..heavy..³ is it?

How much does it ..cost..⁴? ——————→ Price $$$
What's it ..made of..⁵? ——————→ Construction materials
What ..kind of..⁶ fuel does it use / engine does it have? —→ The type or sort
How long does it ..take..⁷ to deliver? ————→ The time required for it to arrive
What sizes / colours does it ..come in..⁸? ————→ Available options
How long will it ..last..⁹? ————→ Durability (how long it remains useful)

6 Complete some more specifications. Use words from the list below.

Resolution ⑨   Capacity ③   Fuel ④
Materials ①   Weight ⑦   Speed ⑩
Pressure ⑤   Memory ⑪   Voltage ⑧
Colours ②   Dimensions ⑫
Maximum water output ⑥

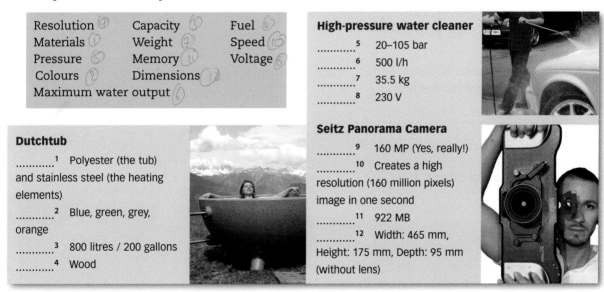

High-pressure water cleaner
..........⁵   20–105 bar
..........⁶   500 l/h
..........⁷   35.5 kg
..........⁸   230 V

Dutchtub
..........¹   Polyester (the tub) and stainless steel (the heating elements)
..........²   Blue, green, grey, orange
..........³   800 litres / 200 gallons
..........⁴   Wood

Seitz Panorama Camera
..........⁹   160 MP (Yes, really!)
..........¹⁰   Creates a high resolution (160 million pixels) image in one second
..........¹¹   922 MB
..........¹²   Width: 465 mm, Height: 175 mm, Depth: 95 mm (without lens)

7 Work with a partner. Ask and answer questions about the products.

A *Tell me about the high pressure water cleaner. What's the pressure?*
B *It's twenty to a hundred and five bar.*

8 🎧 Listen to some more specifications. Make notes.

9 What do the specs in **8** describe? You can check your answer in file 39 on page 103.

10 Play a guessing game with the class.

1 Everyone thinks of an object and writes its specifications or statistics.
2 In turns read your statistics to the class.
3 The class asks for more information (*What's it made of? What's the fuel source?*).
4 Everyone guesses what the object is.

Features and benefits

1 🎧 What unusual features does this bicycle have? How do you think it works? Listen to someone describing it and see if you're right.

2 🎧 Listen again and complete these notes on the bike's features and benefits.

1 It .... approximately 11 kilograms. *weighs*
2 So it's .... lift and move around. *easy to*
3 It .... a spring-loaded mechanism in the *has/allows* rear, which .... the rear wheels to move inwards and outwards.
4 It's more .... than other bikes. *stable*
5 The chain's .... *completely covered*
6 You .... worry about *don't have to* clothing getting caught up in it.

Look at the notes. Which ones describe:
a features – facts about the way the bike is built and how it operates? *1 3 5*
b benefits – helpful and useful things that make this bike better than others? *2, 4, 6*

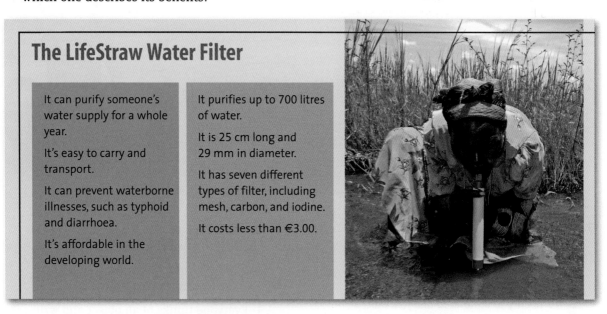

3 Read two descriptions of this invention. Which one describes its features and which one describes its benefits?

The LifeStraw Water Filter

It can purify someone's water supply for a whole year.

It's easy to carry and transport.

It can prevent waterborne illnesses, such as typhoid and diarrhoea.

It's affordable in the developing world.

It purifies up to 700 litres of water.

It is 25 cm long and 29 mm in diameter.

It has seven different types of filter, including mesh, carbon, and iodine.

It costs less than €3.00.

4 Which description:

1 is more technical?
2 explains how the LifeStraw can solve problems?
3 is better for selling the invention, in your opinion? Why?

5 Read the features of another invention. What are its benefits?

The Hypno PQ Tent

The Hypno PQ tent is supported by air, not tent poles.

It comes with a pump and it can be erected in less than a minute.

Its total area is 2.88 m².

It weighs 1.22 kg out of its bag and 1.4 kg when packed.

6 Match the features above to these benefits.

1 Two people can fit comfortably inside this tent. *Total area is 2.88m²*
2 You don't have to use tent poles to erect it. *Supported by air*
3 It's light enough to carry on long walks. *1.22/1.4*
4 It saves time because it's quicker to put up than a normal tent. *Pump*

7 Look at the box below. Which sentences could describe:

1 how something can help you?
2 how it compares to similar products?
3 what it's like?
4 capabilities?

Describing benefits

Many sales professionals say describing benefits (rather than features) makes people want to buy things.

It's *affordable / light / helpful.* (1)
It's *safer / more stable / quicker / less likely to fall over.* (2)
It can *purify ... / prevent ... / save ... .* (3)
It's *easy to erect / move / carry.* (1)
It *allows / helps ... .* (1)
You don't have to ... . (1)

8 Choose an object – any object – in the room you're in now.

1 Describe its features: its composition, size, weight, cost, what it comes with, and so on.
2 Describe its benefits: the problems it solves and why people would want to buy it.

9 Work with a partner. Describe the features and benefits of some more products.

A – Look at file 30 on page 100.
B – Look at file 2 on page 88.

10 Think about a product or service your company provides or a product you know well. What are its features and benefits?

1 What does it allow or help people to do?
2 What problems does it solve or prevent?
3 How does it save energy, time, or money?

(handwritten) ① send audio #6

Giving instructions

1 Have you ever done these things?

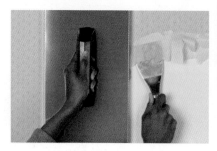

1 Used a wallpaper stripper

2 Laid a garden patio

3 Hypnotized someone

You're going to listen to some instructions for these tasks. Predict some of the words you'll hear. Before you listen, write a list of words for each task.

2 🎧 Listen. Did you hear any of the words you predicted?

3 🎧 Listen again to the instructions for using the wallpaper stripper. Are these things necessary, advisable, or things you shouldn't do? Complete the table.

1 Fill the tank with water.
2 Use distilled water.
3 Wait a few minutes.
4 Start before the light goes on.
5 Touch the plate to see if it's hot.
6 Work downwards.

Necessary	Advisable but not necessary	Things you shouldn't do
1 *3*	*2,6*	*4,5*

4 🎧 Listen again to the instructions for laying a patio. Why do you need to do these things?

1 Make sure the corners are square. *have problems*
2 Excavate to a depth of 12 cm. *8 for gravel/4 for paving*
3 Slope downwards away from the house. *so water will drain off*

5 🎧 Listen again to the instructions for hypnotizing someone and complete the sentences.

1 *First* of all, *make sure* the subject is sitting or lying down.
2 *Once* they've started to relax, tell them to think about their arms.
3 *Be careful* not to speak too fast, *or else* it won't work.
4 *It's important to* talk with a relaxed and soothing voice, and say lots of positive things like *That's right, good, you're doing just fine,* *otherwise* they won't have confidence in you.
5 *After that* move on to other parts of their body.

Sequencing

We often use these words and phrases to indicate the order we need to do things:
Before you begin ... First ... Then ... Next ... After that ...
When indicates one action immediately follows another.
When *the water's hot enough, the light comes on.*
Once suggests one action has to be completed before another can happen.
Once *you've marked out the area, you can start excavating.*

6 Work with a partner and practise using the sequencing expressions.

A – turn to file 3 on page 89.
B – turn to file 38 on page 103.

Explaining why

We can use *otherwise* and *or else* to give warnings.
Slope it downwards. **Otherwise** *the rain water won't run off.*
Make sure you keep the corners square, **or else** *you could hit problems later.*

7 Suggest suitable endings for these sentences.

1 Wait for the drill bit to cool before you remove it. Otherwise ...
2 Don't forget to wrap the parts in bubble wrap before you send them, or else ...
3 Make sure the machine is unplugged before you take the cover off, or else ...
4 It's important to sterilize the instruments before you use them. Otherwise ...
5 Before you switch the lathe on, make sure there's enough coolant, or else ...
6 Don't forget to switch off the pump before you disconnect the pipe. Otherwise ...
7 It's important to write your password down somewhere safe, or else ...
8 Make sure you press the 'save' key before you close the file. Otherwise ...

8 Think of a practical task that you know how to do well. For example:

a changing a flat tyre.
b hanging a roll of wallpaper.
c replacing a broken tile.
d repairing a leaking tap.
e deleting a computer program and installing a new one.
f making a cup of tea.
g sending a text message from your mobile phone.
h something else (your choice).

Prepare to instruct some other students on how to do it. Think about the order they need to do things and any problems they might encounter.

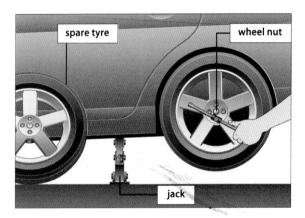

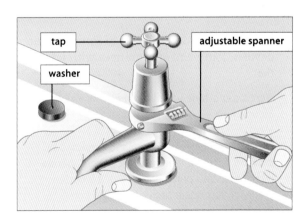

9 Work in groups. Take turns giving your presentations. Listen to your colleagues' presentations and decide:

1 which was the clearest.
2 which was the most useful.
3 which was the most interesting.

Mechanisms

1 How many ways can you think of to put out a candle?

2 How does this candle extinguishing device work?

3 Read this description and label the diagram.

> When you shoot the ball into the basket, it operates the pulley so the watering can pours water into the funnel. The scales push the umbrella up which tilts the wooden platform which pivots. The weight drops onto the bellows which expel air and blow out the candle.

which and *that*

We often join sentences by using *which* in place of *it* or *they*.
This is a watering can. It tilts and pours water into the funnel.
This is a watering can which tilts and pours water into the funnel.

In informal spoken style, we use *that* instead of *which*.
There's a funnel that directs water in to the scales.

4 Improve these descriptions of some similar devices. Join pairs of sentences with *which* or *that*.

Here's a machine which extinguishes candles by blowing air.

> Here's a machine. It extinguishes candles by blowing air. It's a manual device. You operate it by hand. You pull a ring. It tilts a wooden platform. It drops a heavy ball onto some bellows. They are at the end of the bed.

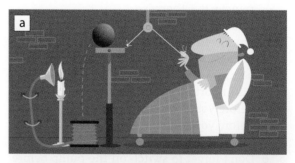

> Here's another device. It's fully automatic. It uses bellows. You position them under the bed. You just get into bed. It depresses the bellows. It forces air along the hose. It blows out your candle.

5 Here are some more devices for extinguishing candles. Label the diagrams with words from the list. Use the definitions to help you.

bellows	belt	boxing glove
broom	cam	chute
fuse	hammer	hook
loop	rocket	scales
spring	tray	wheel

bellows a piece of equipment which blows air

a cam a wheel with a bump that sticks out which changes circular motion to up and down motion, or back and forth motion

a chute a long narrow passage which things slide down

a loop a piece of rope which is shaped like a circle

scales a device which is used to weigh things

a tray a shallow box which has no lid

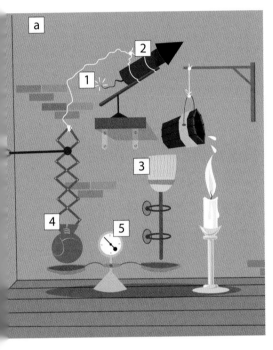

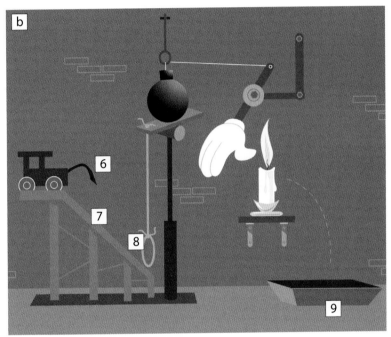

6 Work with a partner. Explain how each device works. How well do you think they operate? Can you suggest any improvements?

7 Work in pairs or groups. Design a similar device for:

1 putting out a candle.
2 scratching your back.
3 making breakfast.

Get ready to present your design to the class and explain how it works.

8 Listen to everyone's presentations. Can you suggest improvements? Decide which team's device was:

1 the most imaginative.
2 the most practical.
3 the funniest.

Jobs

1 Complete these sentences about your job.

1 I work for ....
(*for* + company name, e.g. *Allied Technologies*)
2 I work at ....
(*at* + location, e.g. *at our Lodz factory / site*)
3 I work in ....
(*in* + a department or place, e.g. *logistics / the paint shop*)
4 I work with ....
(*with* + regular contacts, e.g. *the design and purchasing departments*)
5 I'm responsible for ....
(*in charge of* or *responsible for* + responsibilities, e.g. *production planning*)
6 My job involves ....
(*involves* + activity, e.g. *checking / testing / calculating / a lot of travel*, etc.)

2 Work in pairs. Interview one another about your jobs or a job you'd like to have. Say if you need to do these things. Explain why or why not. Listen to your partner carefully and take brief notes.

A	B
1 work in a team	1 travel to customers or suppliers
2 be a good listener	2 read a lot of technical documents
3 give advice	3 be creative
4 design things	4 work with strangers
5 make decisions quickly	5 organize things
6 speak English	6 speak foreign languages

3 Tell the class about your partner's job.

How does it work?

1 Think of some things and substances that catch fire easily or can easily explode.

2 An aerial shell is one of the most popular fireworks in public displays. Read a description of how it works. Label the diagram with words from the list.

fuse	time fuse	bursting charge
stars	casing	lifting charge

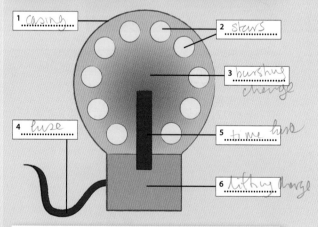

1 *casing*
2 *stars*
3 *bursting charge*
4 *fuse*
5 *time fuse*
6 *lifting charge*

The aerial shell is placed in a small steel pipe, which is called a mortar, for launching. The shell's casing is made of paper which is strengthened with string. It has to be capable of withstanding high pressure because it is launched into the air at high speed.

Size and distance

1 Complete the table.

Dimensions		
Noun	Adjective	Questions
length	long	*How long is it?* *What's the length?*
¹	wide	²
³	high	⁴
depth	⁵	⁶
weight	heavy	*What's the weight?* *How heavy is it?* *How much does it weigh?*

Use *a / an* or *per* to relate two different measures. *Per* is more formal.
My car does 5.5 kilometres a / per litre.

The fuse, which is attached to the base of the aerial shell, consists of a piece of string that has been impregnated with gunpowder and wrapped in a paper tube. When one end is lit, the flame travels to the gunpowder in the base of the shell, which is known as the lifting charge. When it catches fire, it produces hot gases and a sharp increase in pressure which pushes the shell out of the mortar.

The lifting charge also ignites the time fuse, which controls when the shell will burst in the sky. In a small 10 cm shell, the time fuse burns for about two and a half seconds, but with bigger shells, the delay is longer. The delays are timed so the shell breaks at its apogee, which is the point when it is almost motionless in the sky and gravity begins to take over.

When the time fuse goes off, it emits a flash, which sets off the bursting charge. This is the gunpowder inside the shell. The bursting charge explodes the shell and ignites the stars, throwing them in all directions. The stars are a mixture of gunpowder and aluminium and iron filings which produce a bright light and sparks which never fail to have an 'Ahhh' effect on a watching crowd.

2 Work in pairs. Practise asking and answering questions with a partner.

A – Use the information below.
B – Use the information in file 27 on page 98.

A

Ask **B** for the information you need to complete the sentences and answer their questions.

Example
How wide is the English channel at its narrowest point?

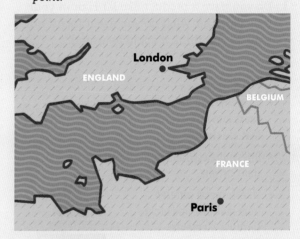

1 The English channel is only 21 mi wide at its narrowest point.
2 The Trans-Canada highway is 7,699 km long.
3 Light travels at a speed of around 3000 km/s
4 Because of cosmic dust falling from space, the Earth's weight increases by about 10 tonnes every day.
5 A human hair is strong enough to lift a weight of 2 kg.
6 The East Rand mine in South Africa is 3.9 km deep.
7 The Taipei 101 building in Taiwan is 508 m high.
8 A redwood tree can grow to a height of over 100 m.
9 The length of a day on Venus is 243 Earth days
10 An Olympic swimming pool is at least 2 m deep.
11 The average weight of a male chimpanzee is 59 kg
12 The Blue Bridge in St Petersburg, Russia, is the widest bridge in the world. It's 97.3 m wide.

Describing fixes

1 Do you have a product like Mr Fixit in your toolbox? If so, what do you use it for? If not, how do you think it could be useful?

Uses

- Keeps moving parts running smoothly. Soaks into rust. Loosens and frees metal parts that are stuck. ③

- Dries out electrical systems and prevents short circuits. ④

- Shields metal surfaces from moisture and other corrosive elements. Prevents rust and corrosion. ②

- Gets under dirt and grease, making it easy to wipe them away. ① Dissolves adhesives, making it easy to remove tape and sticky labels.

2 Here are four things Mr Fixit does. Match each one to a different use.

1 Cleans 　　3 Lubricates
2 Protects 　　4 Displaces moisture

3 Find words or expressions in the uses that mean:

1 clean by rubbing with a soft cloth. *wipe*
2 stops something happening. *prevents*
3 operating efficiently. *running smoothly*
4 makes something become liquid. *dissolves*
5 makes something completely wet. *soaks*
6 guards against, protects. *shields*
7 won't move. *are stuck*

4 Look at the pictures. How could Mr Fixit help in these situations?

lubricate

loosen + free

dissolve

displace moisture

5 (7) Mr Fixit is very popular. Listen to four people talking about how they used it.

1 Match each story to the correct picture.
2 Say what the problem was and explain how Mr Fixit helped.

1 d   2 c   3 b   4 a

6 (7) Listen again and complete the sentences.

1 a I tried turning the key in the .... *ignition*, but it was *so   wet* nothing happened.
   b It stops them *freezing* in cold weather.
2 a We tried *peeling* them, but they were *so firmly stuck*, we couldn't, and they left a *residue*.
   b We sprayed it on and left it to *soak*.
3 a I pulled and twisted it, but it was *so rusty*, it wouldn't *budge*.
   b I gave it one *tug*, and the seat *came out*!
4 a It kept us cool, but it made *so much noise*, we couldn't sleep.
   b My husband *squirted* the moving parts with Mr Fixit, and that *did the trick*.

Explaining effects

We use *so* to add emphasis when we're explaining effects:
*The labels were **so firmly stuck** we couldn't remove them.* ◄
*It was **so rusty** it wouldn't budge.* ◄ ── effects
*The fan made **so much noise** it kept us awake.* ◄

7 Suggest possible endings for these sentences.

1 The door was so firmly shut I couldn't …
2 The machine made so much noise we couldn't …
3 The scissors were so rusty they wouldn't …
4 The string was so tangled he couldn't …
5 The windscreen was so dirty we couldn't …

8 Use the words from the lists to complete some more stories.

2	*3*	*4*	*1*
lubricated	wiped	did	checked

My car's door warning alarm kept going off last week. I ....[1] all the doors, but they were all shut. So today I ....[2] all the door latches. I sprayed lots of Mr Fixit on them and ....[3] the excess off with a rag. It ....[4] the trick, and the door alarm stopped.

7	*6*	*8*	*5*
dissolved	sprayed	peeled	used

A couple of years ago we had a mouse in the kitchen. We ....[5] a sticky strip to catch it but we didn't want to kill it. But the adhesive was so strong we couldn't remove it without hurting it. So we ....[6] Mr Fixit around its feet and it ....[7] the adhesive. Then we ....[8] the mouse off the strip, took it to a field, and let it go.

10	*12*	*9*	*11*
gave	loosened	soaked	squirted

I went away on a trip for six months and when I got home the garbage disposal in my sink was so rusty it wouldn't budge. I ....[9] it in Mr Fixit and left it for a while. A little later I ....[10] it a tug and it moved. I ....[11] on some more Mr Fixit and ....[12] it some more. Then I turned it on and now it's running smoothly again.

9 Work in pairs or groups. Think of something you've had to mend or repair. Explain what the problem was and what you did to fix it.

Explaining processes

1 What's your favourite film? Does it contain any special effects? How do you think they were they created?

2 Read about a movie making process and number the pictures in the correct order.

Chroma Key

The chroma key process is used in the movie industry to create special effects. It enables actors and actresses to look as if they are in dangerous situations, when in fact they're perfectly safe. Here's how it works.

1 First, a green background is created in the studio. Often a wall and floor are painted green, or sometimes a fabric screen is erected. If it's fabric, extra care is taken to ensure that it's smooth and evenly lit.

2 Next, an actor or actress is videoed in the studio against the green background. They could ride a bike, hang from a ladder, or stand on their head, but they can't wear any green clothes. Only the background is green.

3 The video is then taken to the editing room. Because human skin is a warm colour with very few green tones, it's possible to select just the green background and replace it with a transparent layer. This is easily done with video editing software. (Sometimes directors prefer to work with blue instead of green. Both colours work well.)

4 The video is now ready to be combined with a new background scene. This could be a shot of a dangerous location like a fiery volcano, a tall skyscraper, or perhaps a fast-moving river.

5 The background scene is placed 'behind' the actor or actress and the two images are mixed. The director gets the exciting shot they need, but with no risk to the actor, actress, or the movie budget.

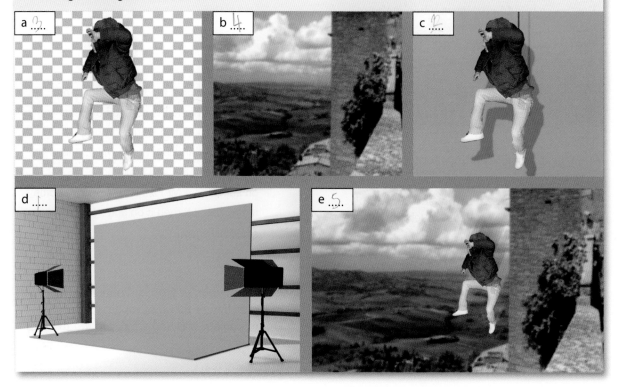

a 3.
b 4.
c 2.
d 1.
e 5.

Active or passive?

When we're interested in what things or people do, we use active forms.
Both green and blue **work** *well.*
The film director **gets** *an exciting shot.*
When we're interested in what happens to things or people, we use passive forms.
The video **is taken** *to the editing room.*
The actors **are videoed** *in the studio.*

3 Find more examples of active and passive forms in the description of the chroma key process. Explain why they are used.

4 What's the best way of continuing after the sentences below? Choose the best alternative. Think about whether you need to say what things do or what's happened to them.

1 I have a new camera.
  a It was made in China.
  b People in China made it.

2 It's very small and compact.
  a It fits in your pocket.
  b It's fitted in your pocket.

3 Did you see the movie *March of the Penguins*?
  a A film crew shot it in Antarctica.
  b It was shot in Antarctica.

4 This mobile phone has a built-in camera.
  a But I'm not sure how it works.
  b But I'm not sure how it's worked.

5 Children love watching animated movies.
  a And lots of adults love watching them, too.
  b And watching them is loved by lots of adults, too.

6 There are many software packages for making 3D animations.
  a People call one of the most powerful ones MAYA.
  b One of the most powerful ones is called MAYA.

7 Sanyo makes a waterproof video camera.
  a It enables you to take shots under water.
  b You're enabled to take shots under water.

8 *The Groovy Movie Picture House* is the world's first mobile solar-powered cinema.
  a Eight large solar panels power it.
  b It's powered by eight large solar panels.

5 Work in pairs or small groups. You are directing a low-budget movie and you need some special effects. You want to create these shots with no risk to your actors or your budget. How can it be done?

1 An actor climbing up a 50 m wall
2 A space ship moving across the sky at night
3 An actor in pouring rain when it's not raining
4 An actor being killed with a long sword
5 The water in a river rising up and parting, so your actors can walk across the river bed

6 Compare your answers with some other groups. Did you have the same ideas? You can read how these things have been done in some real movies in file 31 on page 100.

5 Where are you?

Welcoming visitors

1 Discuss these questions.

1 What kinds of people might visit your place of work or school (suppliers, customers, parents, etc.)?
2 What do visitors have to do when they enter the premises (provide ID, get a badge or visitor's pass, wait at reception, etc.)?

2 🎧 Listen to four conversations with a visitor. Number these sentences in the order you hear them.

a .... Nice to meet you.
b .... It was great meeting you.
c .... Would you like me to give you directions?
d .... I'm afraid I won't get to you by ten.
e .... Take the airport exit.
f .... Do you need a hand?
g .... Could you send an estimate for maintenance, too?
h .... That's very kind of you.

3 Find a sentence in **2** that was used to:

1 give instructions.
2 ask someone to do something.
3 say sorry.
4 thank.
5 offer physical help.
6 offer to do something else.
7 greet.
8 say goodbye.

Suggest ways to respond to the sentences.

4 Complete the table with these phrases. Then think of alternative expressions for doing these things.

I'm afraid …	Yes, of course.
Do you want a hand?	Could you…?
That's very kind of you.	I can manage.
You're welcome.	That's OK.

Asking someone to do something *Can you … ?* ....¹	Saying yes *Sure.* ....²
Thanking *Thanks very much.* ....³	Replying *It's a pleasure.* ....⁴
Offering help *Would you like me to … ?* ....⁵	Saying yes and *no* *Thanks, I'd appreciate it.* ....⁶
Saying you're sorry *I'm sorry but …* ....⁷	Replying *Don't worry about it.* ....⁸

5 Work with a partner. Practise asking for things and responding.

1 You've lost a business contact's email address. Your partner may know it.
2 You don't know how to get to your partner's company.
3 You have no 25-cent coins for a parking meter, but you have a 20-dollar bill.
4 You have to make a call, but your mobile phone's battery is flat.*
5 You only have three copies of a diagram. There will be six people at the meeting.
6 You left the lights of your car on, and now it won't start.

flat **BrE** – dead **AmE**

6 Work with a partner. Practise making offers and responding.

1 A visitor has a lot to carry.

2 Perhaps they're thirsty.

3 They have a headache.

4 They need to get to the station.

7 Work with a partner. Think of ways to say sorry, give excuses, and respond in these situations.

1 Arriving late for a meeting

2 Having to cancel an appointment

3 No tours of your workshop today

4 A late delivery

8 Do we say these things when we're greeting someone or saying goodbye?

1 Let's stay in touch.
2 It's been great seeing you again.
3 What have you been up to?
4 Look forward to seeing you in Milan.
5 It's nice to put a face to a name at last.
6 Long time no see. How are you keeping?
7 Have a safe journey back.

Work with a partner and practise the phrases. Act out two conversations:

1 greeting a business contact.
2 saying goodbye.

9 Work with a partner. Take turns to visit one another's companies. Follow the flow chart.

Visitor	Host
Call your partner and tell them you'll be late.	Tell your visitor what they have to do when they arrive.
Check you understand the instructions. End the call.	Greet your visitor. Ask about their trip and offer help with their bags.
Respond and explain you'll have to leave early because of your flight.	Offer a lift to the airport. Take them to the meeting room.
Respond.	The meeting's nearly over. Ask if your visitor needs any more information.
Ask your host to send you an updated project schedule.	Respond. You have 30 minutes before you must leave for the airport. Offer to show your visitor round the workshops.
Say no. You'd like to get to the airport early. Thank your host for organizing the meeting.	Respond.
Thank your host for driving you to the airport.	Respond. Thank your visitor for coming and for the useful meeting.
Respond. Make arrangements for your future contact.	Respond and say goodbye.

Tracking

1 How many security cameras record your actions during a normal day? What other technologies track your activities?

2 Read about Hank Shaw's morning. How many devices track him?

THE TRACKING OF HANK SHAW

6.40 a.m.
Hank gets up and walks to his local shop. There aren't <u>any</u> other people around at this time in the morning, but closed-circuit television cameras record his journey.

> It's estimated that the UK has one CCTV camera for every 14 people.

7.18 a.m.
Hank buys a newspaper and <u>some</u> chewing gum and pays with his MasterCard. He just waves it near a device at the checkout that reads the data stored on the card's RFID (Radio Frequency Identification) chip. Then he returns home and uses <u>another</u> RFID device as a key to enter his building. <u>The</u> cameras record him again.

> RFID chips don't cost much, so they are becoming common in credit cards, passports, and <u>a lot of</u> items we buy in stores.

7.37 a.m.
Hank turns on his mobile phone and finds two messages. He listens to them both, but neither is important. He has <u>plenty of</u> time, so he checks his email. 'There's <u>loads of</u> spam again', he thinks. He also finds a message from his estate agent, saying 'I see you've been on my website.'

> Mobile phones transmit signals constantly when switched on, and phone companies can trace their approximate location. There are <u>lots of</u> ways to track someone's web-surfing history, especially if they have registered at your site.

7.55 a.m.
Hank doesn't have <u>much</u> time for breakfast, but he has <u>a little</u> milk and cereal while he does <u>a couple of</u> Google searches. Then he does <u>a few</u> more.

> Google receives <u>billions of</u> search queries a month, and uses the data for research. It helps Google to target their ads better.

8.20 a.m.
Hank has very <u>little</u> time to get to work now, so he drives fairly fast. He passes <u>several</u> speed cameras, but fortunately none of them flash. He has a Mercedes-Benz with GPS navigation and a roadside emergency service.

> The Global Positioning System is constantly transmitting signals via satellite. In an emergency, the roadside service company would have precise information about Hank's location.

9.00 a.m.
Another CCTV camera records Hank's arrival at work. He logs on to his company's network. Every keystroke he makes is recorded, along with <u>all</u> the documents and web pages he views. Hank will be tracked many more times today by different technologies.

> <u>Many</u> companies use software programs to monitor their employees' computer use and record their telephone calls. <u>Few</u> people realize quite how much tracking equipment is in use today, but many are concerned about the effects it could have on personal privacy.

3 List the tracking devices in the story.

1 What information does each one store or transmit?
2 How does each one make Hank's life easy or improve security?
3 Could any have a negative impact on safety, security, or personal privacy?

4 Are the underlined words and expressions in the text used with countable nouns [C], uncountable nouns [U], or both [C / U]?

Countable and uncountable nouns

Countable nouns can be singular or plural.
There's a camera.
There are some cameras.
Uncountable nouns can only be singular.
There's some milk.
Some nouns can have two meanings – one countable and one uncountable.
Hank doesn't have much time. [U]
Hank will be tracked many more times today. [C]

5 Look at these nouns from the text. Are they countable [C], uncountable [U], or both [C / U]? Which one is plural?

time	equipment	document
device	information	data
people	research	satellite
email	privacy	technology

6 What's the difference in meaning between these pairs of sentences?

1 a There are loads of tracking devices.
  b There are too many tracking devices.

2 a We have plenty of satellites.
  b We have several satellites.

3 a Turn off all the cameras.
  b Turn off both the cameras.

4 a Neither of the speed cameras work.
  b None of the speed cameras work.

5 a There's a little time to eat and relax.
  b There's little time to eat and relax.

Check your answers in file 40 on page 103.

little / few vs. *a little / a few*

A little and *a few* indicate small quantities.
We have a little extra time, so let's relax for a few minutes.
Little and *few* have a rather negative meaning. They often indicate an insufficient quantity.
Few people understand this. We have little time to do all the things we need to do.

7 Complete these sentences with *a little*, *a few*, *little*, or *few*.

1 We installed a CCTV system in the loading area ………. days ago.
2 We should have ………. time to do some sightseeing after the meeting.
3 Very ………. money was allocated for the project, so I'm not surprised it failed.
4 We could improve the fuel efficiency by making ………. small design changes.
5 The job wasn't advertised, so ………. people applied for the position.
6 Allen can speak ………. Portuguese. He worked in Brazil for six months.
7 Unfortunately, we have ………. test results.
8 The research was conducted several years ago, so the data will be ………. use to us now.

8 Do you agree or disagree with these statements? Work in pairs or groups and discuss your opinions.

1 More CCTVs should be installed in urban areas.
2 Intelligence agencies should be allowed to monitor everyone's PCs.
3 Companies should not monitor their employees' phone calls, emails, or web activity.
4 It would be good if everyone carried an RFID that stored details of their medical history, blood group, any medication they are currently taking, and so on.
5 Children should wear GPS tracking devices so their parents can monitor their movements.
6 Only terrorists and criminals have anything to fear from modern surveillance technologies.

6 Looking ahead

Planning

1 Read the information on Franklin Furnaces.

1 What does the company do?
2 What do its start-up technicians do?
3 Do you think you'd like to work for this company as a start-up technician? (Why / Why not?)

> With more than 45 years of experience and installations in 86 countries, Franklin Furnace Co., Inc., has developed an international reputation for excellence. We will design and construct the furnace that meets your specific requirements. Our qualified start-up technicians will guide the installation on your site and perform adjustments, prior to giving hands-on training to your operators and maintenance crews. With Franklin Furnace, you can have the highest level of quality control and confidence that your equipment will be assembled and installed correctly.

2 🎧 Franklin Furnace Co., Inc., has sold a furnace to a customer in China. Listen to two start-up technicians planning their trip. What potential problems do they discuss? Make notes.

3 🎧 Listen again. Then complete these sentences.

1 If the site isn't ready, it ....
2 If there's no 240-volt electricity supply, the customer ....
3 If the platform isn't strong enough, they ....
4 If a tool they need is missing, they ....
5 If that takes too long, they ....

4 Work with a partner. Make similar conversations about other things the start-up technician's worried about.

Example
A *What'll we do if we don't like our hotel?*
B *Don't worry. We'll find another one.*

1 don't like our hotel
2 there's nobody to meet us at the airport
3 don't have all the parts we need
4 don't understand the Chinese installation engineers
5 don't get along with the Chinese engineers
6 the equipment documentation isn't ready
7 our mobile phones don't work in China
8 don't like the food
9 get food poisoning
10 don't have enough time to do the job

5 🎧 Listen to some more of the conversation and answer these questions.

1 Why does the technician want to get to the airport early?
2 Why does she want to have lunch there?

If, unless, and in case

We use *if* to talk about future possibilities:
If my husband's busy, I'll take the train.

Unless has a similar meaning to *if ... not*.
My husband will drive me to the airport unless he's busy.

We use *in case* to talk about precautions we must take to stop something bad from happening.
I like to get there early in case there are queues at security.

6 What's the difference in meaning between these pairs of sentences?

1 I'll be there at 8.30 if I miss the 7 o'clock train.
I'll be there at 8.30 unless I miss the 7 o'clock train.

2 Leave home early if the traffic's bad.
Leave home early in case the traffic's bad.

7 Complete these sentences using your own ideas.

1 You'd better take your ID card in case …
2 The machine won't start unless …
3 If we don't upgrade our software soon, …
4 You'd better check that order in case …
5 Sorry, but if I don't write those details down now, …
6 I can't get to sleep at night unless …
7 We'd better not park here in case …
8 Unless we find a petrol station soon, …
9 If we don't take all the tools we need, …

Done 1/8/22

8 You have accepted this job with Franklin Industrial Furnace Co., Inc.

WANTED

Start-up engineers and technicians for an installation project next February in Dalandzadgad, Mongolia. The assignment will last for approximately 4 weeks. Good rates of pay.

Work in pairs or groups. Discuss these questions and write a list of items you'd like to take with you.

1 The installation site is in the Gobi desert. The temperature will vary between -15 °C and -35 °C in February. What will you need to take to keep warm?

2 Some Mongolians understand Russian but few speak English. How will you communicate with the Mongolian team if they don't speak much English?

3 How will you communicate with your company, family, and friends if there's no internet access? And what will you do if your mobile phones don't work?

4 Dalandzadgad has a post office, two hotels, a market, and a restaurant that shuts at weekends. It has no electrical or building material stores, but there's a bank, whose manager speaks a little English and an airport with an unpaved runway. Flights arrive from the capital, Ulaanbaatar, every two or three days. What will you do if you need extra parts or tools?

5 What'll you do to entertain yourselves in the evenings?

6 Many Mongolian hospitals are short of basic items including drugs and spare parts for medical equipment. What will you do if someone falls ill or has an accident?

7 Someone told you to watch out for dangerous snakes. What'll you do if you see one?

9 Compare the items on your list with some other students and explain why you want to take those items. Who had the best ideas?

Ulaanbaatar

MONGOLIA

Dalandzadgad

Making comparisons

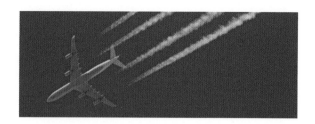

1 How could spending your holiday at home reduce your impact on the environment? Read the text and find out if you're right.

Stay home this summer

Carbon dioxide (CO_2) speeds up global warming, and one of the biggest threats to the environment is the 26 billion metric tonnes of carbon dioxide that humans generate each year. The average European emits around ten metric tonnes of CO_2, and for the average American, the figure's much higher.

Our carbon footprint is a calculation of the CO_2 we emit, and almost everything we do increases it – from turning on our coffee maker to using our mobile phone.

Travelling by car is bad, and flying is much worse, but it's not a simple calculation. Kilometres per passenger, a plane journey produces roughly the same amount of CO_2 as a car journey, or slightly less if it's a large car. But cars are less harmful because the distances people travel by plane tend to be much greater. An average long-haul flight generates 4 tonnes of CO_2 per passenger. And because CO_2 is emitted higher up in the atmosphere, it does more damage.

So one of the most effective things we can do to reduce our carbon footprint is take fewer flights. Why not take your holiday at home this year?

2 Choose the correct word below.

1 CO_2 is (bad/worse) for the environment because it speeds up global warming.
2 Generally speaking, Americans have a (large / larger) carbon footprint than Europeans.
3 A large car emits (more / less) CO_2 per kilometre per passenger than a plane.
4 Car journeys are less damaging to the environment than plane journeys because passengers usually travel (fewer / lower) kilometres.
5 One of the (best / good) ways to reduce our impact on the environment is to take our holidays at home.

3 Complete the language notes. Use the words and phrases from the list.

worse	less	the biggest
fewer	far	the best
less harmful	slightly	

Comparing two or three things

With short adjectives, add *-er / -est* to form comparatives and superlatives.
high – higher – the highest
big – bigger – ....bigger...........[1]

With long adjectives, use *more / most* or *less / least*.
effective – more effective – the most effective
harmful – ......less harmful......[2] *– the least harmful*

Remember! These common adjectives are irregular:
good – better – ......the best......[3]
bad – ......worse......[4] *– the worst*

Comparing quantities

Use *more* and *most* with countable or uncountable nouns.
more kilometres, the most CO_2
Use *less / least* with uncountable nouns. Use *fewer / fewest* with countable nouns.
We can generate ......less......[5] CO_2 *by taking* ......fewer......[6] *flights.*

Describing the size of difference

Use *much, far,* or *a lot* to describe a big difference and *a little, a bit,* or *slightly* to describe a small one.
The figure is much higher. It's ......far......[7] *higher. It's a lot higher.*
The figure is a little lower. It's a bit lower. It's ......slightly......[8] *lower.*

4 Does your country appear in this bar chart? If so, where does it fall? If not, where do you think it would be?

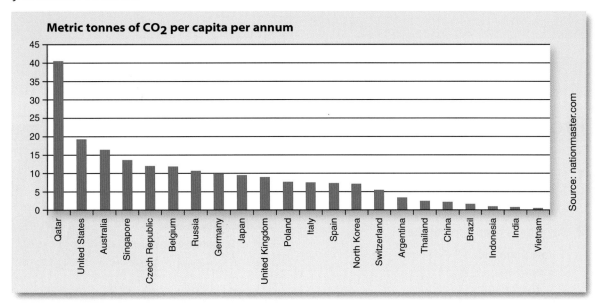

Metric tonnes of CO_2 per capita per annum

Source: nationmaster.com

5 Are these statements true (T) or false (F)? Correct the ones that are wrong. Compare your answers with another student. Did any of the statistics surprise you?

1 People in Qatar produce the least CO_2. F
2 The USA has the highest CO_2 emissions per capita and Indonesia has the lowest. F
3 The average Chinese person has roughly the same carbon footprint as someone from Thailand. T
4 The carbon footprint of someone in the Czech Republic is slightly bigger than the carbon footprint of someone in Singapore. F
5 People in India produce much less CO_2 than people in Russia. T
6 CO_2 emissions from Poland are far worse than CO_2 emissions from Italy. F

6 Here are some more actions we could take to reduce our carbon footprint. Which would have the greatest impact? Rank them from 1 (most effective) to 5 (least effective).

a Using a non-powered mechanical lawn mower that we push to mow the grass. 3
b Eating meat-free meals every other day. 1
c Removing ourselves from junk mail lists so we don't receive unwanted letters in the post. 2
d Switching to reusable cleaning products like sponges instead of paper towels. 5
e Buying books from used book stores or borrowing them from our friends instead of buying new ones. 4

You can check your answers in file 35 on page 101.

7 Work in pairs or groups. Think of more things we can do as individuals to reduce our carbon footprint. Write a list.

Examples
take fewer flights
install more insulation in our homes

8 Look at your list and discuss:

1 Which actions would have the greatest impact on global warming?
2 Which methods of reducing carbon emissions would you find the most difficult to implement?
3 Which things have you already tried?
4 CO_2 emissions speed up global warming. What signs of global warming are you the most concerned about?

Processes

1 Number the steps in the processes in the correct order.

2 Say what's been done to the:

1 raw diamond.
2 steel bars.
3 coffee beans.

Example
First the raw diamonds are mined and then ...

a ...3... pressed
b ...1... heated
c ...2... rolled

a ...4... mounted
b ...3... polished
c ...1... mined
d ...2... cut

a ...3... roasted
b ...4... ground
c ...1... picked
d ...2... dried

Socializing

Match the sentences on the left with a suitable response on the right.

1 How are you doing? g
2 Send my regards to Sue when you see her. e
3 OK, let's stop here and have some coffee. i
4 I was promoted to team leader last week. a
5 I'm afraid I can't make Tim's farewell do on Friday. c
6 Oops! I'm sorry. j
7 More wine? b
8 Could you pass the ketchup? d
9 I studied at Redhill Technical College. f
10 Do you want a lift to the station? h

a Well done. Congratulations.
b No thanks. I'm fine.
c Oh, that's a pity.
d Yes, of course. Here you are.
e Thanks, I will.
f Really? That's a coincidence. So did I.
g Oh, not too bad, thanks. And how are things with you?
h No thanks. A walk will do me good.
i Yes, that sounds like a good idea.
j That's OK. No harm done.

Carbon footprint

1 Work in pairs or small groups and test your knowledge of carbon footprints with this quiz.

Carbon footprint quiz

As individuals we can do a lot to reduce our own CO_2 emissions. But to make better decisions, we need to know what actions will have the biggest impact. Take this quiz and find out how much you know.

1 Which adjustment to a water heater will have a larger impact on CO_2 emissions?

  a reducing the temperature setting from 60 °C to 49 °C

  b insulating the heater

2 Here are two environmentally-friendly ways to do your laundry. Which one will lower your CO_2 emissions more?

  a Always washing clothes in cold water instead of hot.

  b Hanging clothes out to dry instead of using a tumble dryer for six months of the year.

3 Here are some more actions you can take to prevent CO_2 from being released into the atmosphere. Which one is the most effective? Which one is the least effective?

  a Switching things off – so shutting down computers, disconnecting devices like stereos, coffee pots, and TVs, and unplugging mobile phones once they are charged.

  b Taking better care of your refrigerator. Regular maintenance like cleaning the coils and defrosting makes it more efficient. Positioning it in a cool place helps it stay cool. Waiting for hot food to cool down before you store it helps, too.

  c Adjusting the thermostat on your air conditioning unit so that it's half a degree warmer in the summer and lowering the thermostat on your central heating by half a degree in the winter.

2 Turn to file 42 on page 104 to check your answers.

3 Work in pairs or groups and discuss these questions.

  1 Which quiz answers were the most surprising?

  2 Which ways of reducing carbon emissions were the most effective?

  3 Were any of the alternatives less effective than you thought?

4 Which is more valuable for preventing global warming?

  a eating locally grown, unprocessed food once a week

  b planting a tree

5 Which of these actions would have the biggest effect on CO_2 emissions from your home?

  a Replacing three incandescent light bulbs with compact fluorescent bulbs.

  b Buying fewer products that come with lots of packaging so you reduce your garbage by 10%.

  c Installing double-glazed windows, made up of two glass panels with a space in between.

7 Can you explain?

Rules and regulations

1 Have you ever driven a car in another country? Do you know any driving rules that are different in other countries?

send

2 (11) Listen to a traveller renting a car in France. What does she find out about these things?

① cost €15

extra ins needed in Spain

return car by 6:30 Friday

Motorways

Many drinks 1 glas a single beer

return with full tank

4 Here are some of the verbs you heard in the conversation. Write them in the correct list.

see teacher book

must	mustn't	can
can't	have to	don't have to
have got to	should	shouldn't
need to	don't need to	are allowed to
ought to	are not allowed to	

3 Choose the correct verb to complete the sentences.

1 She (has to / is allowed to) pay €15 if she wants the map.
2 If it's wet, she (should / isn't allowed to) drive faster than 110 km/h on a motorway.
3 The information is in the folder, so she (mustn't / doesn't have to) write it down.
4 The French police (can / shouldn't) confiscate her licence on the spot.
5 She (has to / can't) take the car to Spain for a few days.
6 As long as she stays in the EU, she (mustn't / doesn't need to) take out extra insurance.
7 She (must / ought to) return the car with a full tank of petrol if she can.
8 She (can / has got to) drink one glass of wine and stay under the limit.

Permission and obligation verbs	
1 Possible, permitted *are allowed to*	2 Impossible, prohibited
3 Necessary, obligatory	4 Not necessary
5 Correct, a good idea	6 Incorrect, a bad idea

5 Work in pairs or groups. Make a list of some of the things you're permitted and obliged to do when you take a flight. Try to use all the permission and obligation verbs in **4**.

At check in

number of hours before the flight, number of bags, size of luggage, weight of luggage, visas and passports

On the plane

baggage, seat belts, movies, electronic equipment, lavatory, security information

At security

trays, shoes, cigarette lighters, laptops, liquids, sharp objects, medicines, pacemakers

At immigration

queues, stretch your legs, visas, forms

Waiting for departure

smoking, what you can and can't buy, free wi-fi internet access, knives and forks if you eat, duty free allowances

At baggage claim and customs

wait, check tags, pay for a trolley, green / red channels, vegetables and fruit, alcohol, tobacco, perfume

6 Compare your rules with some other groups. Who thought of the most rules? Who had the most interesting rules? Did you all agree?

7 Work in pairs. Read the roles below and act out the conversation.

A – A foreign colleague is coming to live and work in your country for a year. They want to learn about your customs and laws. Answer their questions.

B – You are moving to **A**'s country, where you will live and work for a year. Ask **A** questions and find out as much as you can about:
- driving rules and regulations (speed limits, alcohol limits, age limits, overtaking, parking, etc.).
- customs for tipping in taxis, restaurants, hairdressers, and so on.
- company rules – hours of work, holidays, the dress code, and so on.
- anything else you're interested in.

Equipment documentation

1 Look at the contents page of a user's manual. Write these headings in the correct spaces.

a Routine maintenance procedures
b Equipment set-up
c Operating instructions
d Trouble-shooting guide
e Product functions and controls

CONTENTS

2 On which page could you find out about:

1 who to call if things go wrong?
2 where switches and buttons are and what they do?
3 how much oil and water the machine needs?
4 how to put the equipment together?
5 things you should do to prevent accidents?

3 What's the difference between *routine maintenance* and *a maintenance routine*? Which one is:

a a routine you follow to maintain something, for example *first we replace any worn parts, then we check oil levels* ...?
b maintenance that you perform on a regular basis?

Noun phrases

We often put a noun (the name of a thing) in front of another noun in English. The first noun generally describes the second one.
Routine maintenance = a kind of maintenance
Maintenance routine = a kind of routine
We can add more nouns to the chain. The final noun is generally described by the other nouns.
Routine maintenance procedures = kinds of procedures
The first noun is usually singular.
12-month warranty   NOT ~~12-months warranty~~

4 Explain the difference between *test equipment* and *an equipment test*.

5 What noun phrase could describe these things?

Example
Fluids that are used for lubrication = lubrication fluids

1 A guarantee that lasts for ten years
2 A pipe that's made of steel
3 Adjustments you can make to controls
4 A car that has four doors

5 Instructions for handling equipment
6 Warnings about hazards
7 A hose that's three metres long
8 A manual on operating a machine for users

6 Work with a partner. Look at the manual contents page again and take turns explaining the meanings of some different items. Your partner must name them.

Example
A *The overview of the design of a system*
B *System design overview. OK. Directions for assembling the equipment ...*

7 Work in pairs or teams. Combine the nouns below to name useful pieces of equipment. You can use nouns more than once. The team with the most at the end of two minutes are the winners.

Example
alarm clock

| alarm | headset | clock | bell | radio | telephone | bicycle | door | internet | fire |

8 Look at the pictures.

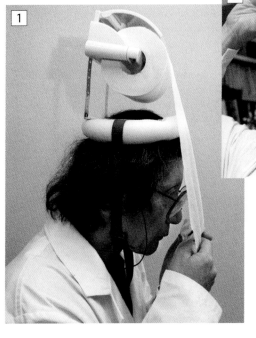

1 Match these names to the devices.
   a Hay-fever relief hat
   b Eye-drop funnel glasses
2 What problem do they try to solve?
   Do you think they could be useful?
   (Why / Why not?)

9 Work in pairs or groups. Read the names of four more devices.
   a Office equipment holder necktie
   b Floor duster baby clothes
   c Back itch relief T-shirt
   d Hands-free umbrella head belt

1 What do you think they could help users do?
2 What do you think they could look like? Draw sketches.

10 Turn to file 12 on page 92 and compare your ideas with the real thing.

8 Take care

Causes and results

1 Look at the pictures. Are these people working efficiently? What health and safety risks can you see? Could they result in:

a broken or fractured bones?
b RSI (repetitive strain injuries)?
c back problems?
d something else? (What?)

2 Ergonomics is the study of ways in which equipment can help people work safely and efficiently. Read a text about ergonomics. Which two pictures does it refer to?

On a well-designed work station, the controls used most often are located within easy reach. The goal is to eliminate any non-essential movements. Poorly designed work stations are not only inefficient, they also can cause discomfort and lead to injuries. In this picture, the user's chair is adjustable and provides good back support. However, the lack of support for the wrist or elbow could result in RSI.

Many injuries and accidents result from lifting. Wherever possible, lifting equipment should be employed to transport heavy loads. When this is impractical, workers should be trained in lifting techniques. Here we can see a worker placing unnecessary strain on their back. The load should be transported by cart or divided between two buckets so it can be balanced. While some accidents are caused by laziness, very often they are due to a lack of training or poor organization of the work flow.

3 The prefix *in-* has a negative meaning (*efficient / inefficient*). Find more prefixes with negative meanings in the text.

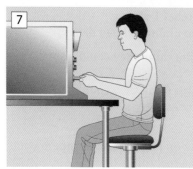 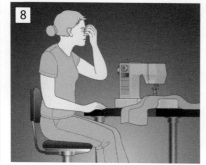 

4 Add an appropriate prefix to complete these sentences.

1 Many workplace injuries are due to .....sufficient or .....proper training.
2 .....adequate ventilation leads to fatigue, and so does equipment that requires .....natural and .....necessary movements.
3 Many fatal and .....fatal accidents result from poorly designed tools.
4 Working .....stop also results in fatigue. Breaks should be provided.
5 A .....organized workplace is an .....safe workplace.

Think of a few more words that begin with the prefixes *in-*, *non- dis-*, *un-*, and *im-*.

Causes and results

Poor design can **cause** *discomfort. Discomfort can* **be caused by** *poor design.*
Laziness can **lead to** *accidents. Some accidents* **are due to** *laziness.*
Lack of training can **result in** *injuries. Injuries can* **result from** *lack of training.*

3 People entering the loading bay have sometimes been knocked over by people leaving.

4 Fire doors are being propped open.

5 Several people have fallen over this step in the reception area.

5 Work with a partner. Describe some of the pictures in **1** in terms of causes and results.

Examples
Carrying heavy loads can cause back strain.
Back strain can be caused by carrying heavy loads.

Suggest ways to prevent the problems.

Example
The worker should be trained to balance the load.

6 Turn to file 1 on page 88.

7 Work in pairs or groups. Read about some workplace problems and discuss ways to solve them.

1 The crane operators don't like the new remote controls.

2 Some drivers are confused by this sign. Someone drove a petrol tanker the wrong way through the car park last week and collided with a truck.

6 A worker in the welding shop was injured in an explosion last week.

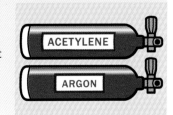

8 What things can cause health and safety problems in your school or workplace? How can you reduce the risks?

Reporting accidents

1 🎧 Listen to a recording of an accident. What do you think happened?

2 Read the witness report and find out if you were right.

3 A health and safety officer interviewed the witness about the accident. Put these words in the correct order and write the questions they asked.

1 did accident happen the when?
When did the accident happen?

2 Mr Patterson at where time the was?

....

3 was doing what he?

....

4 first the switch did machine off he?

....

5 caused the circuit what short?

....

6 the when got what shock happened he electric?

....

7 the did do paramedics what?

....

4 Work with a partner. Act out the interview. Use the questions in **3**.

Past Continuous and Past Simple
Use the Past Continuous to set the scene and describe the situation. He **was trying** to clear a paper jam. He **was wearing** a wedding ring. Use the Past Simple to describe short completed actions or events. He **got** an electric shock. He **hit** his head on a cupboard. Use the Past Simple for actions that interrupted longer actions or happened later. He was trying to clear the jam when he **got** a shock. I **called** for help.

ACCIDENT WITNESS REPORT

Date, Time & Location of Accident:
8.35 a.m., 27 Feb, Building 045, Room 116

Name & Phone No. of Witnesses:
Elaine Jenkins, ext. 1489,
Margaret Down, ext. 1486

Describe the accident in detail (explain the situation and exactly what happened):

Christopher Patterson was trying to clear a paper jam from the photocopier in room 116, but he did not switch off the machine first. He was wearing a wedding ring and we think that caused a short circuit. He got an electric shock which threw him backwards, and he hit his head on a cupboard.

We called for an ambulance. When the paramedics arrived, they bandaged his hand and took him to Brighton Hospital for observation.

5 Complete these descriptions of some more accidents. Use the Past Simple or the Past Continuous.

Example
He *fell* (fall) asleep while he *was driving* (drive).

1 I .... (carry) the box to my workbench when I .... (trip) over a cable.
2 The bottle .... (explode) while I .... (open) it. It .... (cut) my arm.
3 He .... (talk) on his mobile phone and he .... (not pay) attention to the road. He .... (drive) into a tree.
4 She .... (try) to reach something on the top shelf when she .... (knock) the bottle of acid over with her elbow. It .... (spill) down her arm.

5 He .... (slip) and .... (fall) when he .... (repair) the roof. We .... (have to) call an ambulance.
6 A titanium part .... (catch) fire and .... (cause) serious damage.
7 We .... (want) to save time so we weren't using the safety guards. It .... (be) a mistake. Jim .... (wear) a long-sleeved shirt and some of the fabric .... (get) caught up in the rollers.

6 Look at the pictures. What accidents could happen here? Say what happened next.

7 🔊 Listen and find out if you were correct. Make sentences with the Past Continuous and Past Simple. Explain what happened.

8 🎧 Work in pairs or groups.

1 Listen to another accident.
2 Discuss what happened. Prepare to tell the class your version of the story.
3 Listen to everyone else's story and tell them yours. Are they exactly the same?
4 Write a short witness report. Use the report in **2** as a model. One person writes and the other checks spelling and grammar.

Materials

1 Work in pairs. Write a list of some things that are often made of:

steel	wool	silver	concrete
cardboard	wood	ceramic	plastic
polystyrene	glass	leather	foam rubber
cotton	wax	rubber	silicone

2 Why are these materials used? What properties do they have?

 Example
Steel is strong and hard, so it's often used to construct the framework of tall buildings.

3 You're going to read a blog about smart materials. Before you read, look at the photos.

1 What do you think the materials are?
2 What do you think they can do?

Read the blog and find out if you were right.

4 Work with a partner and discuss the materials.

1 Which material do you think would be the most useful and why?
2 Can you think of any more applications for these materials?

Matt's Smart Materials Blog

Welcome! You've come to the best place on the web to find the smartest new materials around – materials with built-in intelligence. So read, explore, and post a comment. Tell me how you think you could use them.

You know how a sponge expands in water? This thin, transparent film does the opposite. When you put it in water, it contracts. It's soft and pliable so it could be used to make the heel straps on flippers when you go swimming. Then when you got into the sea, they'd shrink to fit your feet. Or you could make a rescue rope with it. When it got wet, the rope would shrink and you'd be able to pull people out of the water. Would that be cool or what?

This fabric's really smart. When it's dry, the tiny spikes on its surface stand up, and it's porous. When it's wet, they close and it becomes impervious. The spikes also curl up in extreme temperatures to trap air and provide insulation. It'd make a great raincoat to wear in either winter or summer.

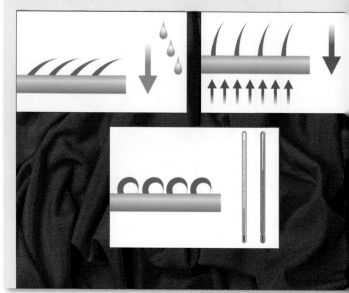

5 Match these adjectives to their meanings.

1	transparent	a	able to last a long time
2	pliable	b	hard, but easily broken
3	porous	c	has a high mass to volume ratio
4	impervious	d	easy to bend without breaking, flexible
5	durable	e	light can pass through it
6	brittle	f	clear, allows you to see through it
7	translucent	g	doesn't allow any liquid or gas to pass through
8	dense	h	has many small holes that allow water and air to pass through slowly

Look back at the materials in **1**. What other materials could have these properties?

Concrete is soft when newly mixed, but it becomes very hard when it sets. It's durable, but it isn't normally something that brightens the room. This stuff is different. It's made from layers of concrete and optical fibres and it's translucent. Imagine living in a building where light comes from the walls. Or imagine a motorway where the layout of the lanes was changed by switching on lights in the ground. And what about dance classes where lights on the floor could show you where to put your feet? Fun stuff, huh?

This dense, impact-absorbing silicone has important safety applications. It's only an inch thick, but you can drop an egg on it and the egg won't break. It could be used to make car bumpers that would absorb the impact of a crash. Or you could put it under baby's crib, or in a children's play ground area. I'd like to install it in my kitchen. Then I'd be able to drop brittle objects like plates without breaking them.

6 Look at Matt's blog again. Find examples of *would* and *could*.

1 What's the contracted form of *would*?
2 When do we use these words?

7 Work in pairs or groups. Think of some unusual uses for these objects.

Example
A brick
You could use it as a door stop. It'd stop a door from closing.
You could put it in your toilet tank. You wouldn't use so much water when you flush.

1	A brick	6	A coil of wire
2	An old tyre	7	An oil drum
3	An empty biscuit tin	8	A fish tank
4	A bed sheet	9	A garden hose
5	A space blanket	10	Some wire coat hangers

Inventions

1 Name these inventions. Then think of ten more great inventions. Which ones would you hate to live without? Brainstorm a list.

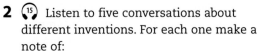

2 (15) Listen to five conversations about different inventions. For each one make a note of:

1 what the invention is.
2 whether the speakers are looking at a prototype of the invention or just imagining it.
3 how the invention works (or could work if it were built).

3 Here are some words from the conversations. Match each one to the correct definition.

detonator	motion detector	drowsiness
set off	scary	withdraw
violent	filter	burst
give up		

1 A material with lots of small holes that's used to block dirt
2 Stop doing something that you'd done regularly before
3 An instrument for discovering or finding movement
4 Frightening
5 Make something start to work
6 Something that begins or causes an explosion
7 Take out, remove
8 The feeling of being sleepy
9 Using physical strength to hurt someone
10 Break open suddenly because of too much pressure

4 (15) Listen to the conversations again and discuss these questions.

1 Do any of these inventions already exist?
2 Can you see any reasons why any of these inventions might not work?
3 Which invention do you think sounds most useful?

5 Match each beginning with a suitable ending to make some sentences about the inventions.

1 If you get sleepy, a it'd call the police.
2 If you typed in the emergency number, b the detonator will explode.
3 If you wave your hand in front of it, c you could drive over them smoothly.
4 If you were going at the correct speed, d an alarm will go off.
5 If it burns down to the filter, e the alarm will stop ringing.

Which invention is each sentence describing?

6 Compare these sentences. What's the difference in meaning?

If you get sleepy, an alarm will go off.
If you got sleepy, an alarm would go off.

Real and unreal possibilities

We use both first and second conditional forms to refer to future possibilities. First conditional forms are used to talk about real possibilities.
*If it **burns** down to the filter, the detonator **will** explode.*
(I think it could burn down.)

We use second conditional forms with *would* and past tenses to talk about situations we think are unreal or imaginary.
*If it **burnt** down to the filter, the detonator **would** explode.*
(I don't think it will burn down.)

7 Look at these events and decide whether they are:

a possible.
b possible in theory, but unlikely to happen in practice.

1 You gain a little weight.
2 The Earth is hit by a very large meteorite.
3 Someone steals your identity.

4 You have some free time this evening.
5 Your English improves.
6 You have difficulty finding a place to park tomorrow.
7 You buy a new car next year.
8 Fuel prices increase to a point that you cannot afford to drive a car.
9 You have difficulty falling asleep tonight.
10 You finish work on time tomorrow.
11 You get a promotion.
12 Your boss gives you a big pay rise.
13 You win a lot of money in a competition.
14 Your English teacher gives you some homework at the end of this lesson.

8 Work with a partner. Compare your answers. If the events in **7** are possible, say what'll happen. If they are possible but unlikely, say what'd happen.

Examples
If I gain a little weight, I'll have to cut back on carbohydrates.
If the Earth were hit by a very large meteorite, I'd be lucky to survive.

9 Work in small groups. You have some money to invest in developing a new invention.

1 Take turns to present different inventions to the group. Inventions can be found in files 4, 7, 10, 14, and 22 at the back of the book.

2 Consider these questions:

a Which invention would be most practical and useful? (Why?)
b Which would be cheapest and easiest to produce?
c Which would make the most money? (Why?)

3 Compare your decision with some other groups. Did you all agree on the same invention?

Future possibilities

1 Discuss these questions in pairs or groups.

  1 Are these things likely to happen in the next ten years? (Why / Why not?)
  2 If they happen or were to happen, what impact will / would they have on our lives? Make sentences with *if*.

  1 The population of the world grows to over 10 billion (It's currently 6.6 bn).
  2 We run out of oil and natural gas.
  3 Governments introduce a CO_2 tax.
  4 Speech recognition software replaces administrative assistants.
  5 Your company decides to outsource some of its activities.
  6 Trains are developed that can travel at supersonic speeds.
  7 More than half the world's population have access to the internet.
  8 The paperless office becomes a reality.
  9 Mandarin becomes the world's most important second language.
  10 Fifty per cent of the working population telecommutes from home.

2 Report back to the class. Be ready to explain:

  1 why you think things are possible or not.
  2 what their impact might be.

3 If you had $1 bn to improve the planet, would you invest in:

  1 renewable energy sources like wind power, hydro power, solar power, and tidal energy?
  2 education and training projects in developing countries?
  3 technologies for recycling waste?
  4 something else? (What?)

Causes and results

1 Work in pairs or groups. Brainstorm the possible causes and results of the problems below.

  a Energy costs have increased by over 20% in the last six months.
  b Twenty-five per cent of the staff at your company are off sick at the moment.
  c Your IT network has been down for the last two days.

2 Choose one of the problems and write an email to one of your customers or a colleague explaining what the causes and results are.

Explaining uses

Work in pairs. Take turns to be **A** and **B**.

A – This is your attic. You don't like to throw anything away because you never know when it could come in handy. If **B** suggests throwing something out, tell them about the useful properties it has and why you think you should keep it.

B – If **A** cleared out their attic, there would be all kinds of things they could do with the space. Suggest they throw some things away.
Begin:
Why don't you throw away this …

Airport rules

1 Where might you see signs like these? According to the signs, which sentences are correct? You may choose more than one.

1

a You're not allowed to pay tax when you shop here.
b If you're travelling outside the EU, you can buy tax free goods here.
c EU travellers mustn't pay tax.
d You don't have to pay tax if you're travelling outside the EU.

2

a You've got to keep your bags with you at all times.
b You should check in all your bags.
c You mustn't leave your bags anywhere.
d Your bags can be destroyed if you leave them somewhere.

3

a You ought to get your travel documents out of your bag.
b You're allowed to show your travel documents.
c You needn't show your travel documents.
d You should get ready to show your travel documents.

1 DUTY FREE SHOPPING
For passengers travelling to countries outside the EU.

2 Keep bags with you at all times. Unattended bags may be destroyed.

3 Please have your boarding pass and passport ready.

2 Complete these sentences with *mustn't* or *don't have to*.

1 I .... forget to pack my passport.
2 They're calling our flight. Hurry up! We .... be late!
3 We've got plenty of time. You .... rush.
4 It's a direct flight. We .... change planes.
5 You .... take out insurance, but it's a good idea.
6 All this security is a nuisance, but we .... complain.

10 What's cooking?

Explaining how

1 Would you like to try making this recipe? (Why / Why not?)

Carbonated strawberries

Begin by cutting some strawberries in half and placing them, cut-side-up, on a plate. Next, get a large container and half fill it with dry ice. Dry ice is the solid form of carbon dioxide (CO_2). The interesting thing about dry ice is it has no liquid form. Instead of melting, it sublimes, which means it changes directly from a solid form to carbon dioxide gas.

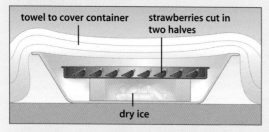

towel to cover container   strawberries cut in two halves

dry ice

You want the strawberries to rest on the dry ice without touching it, so lay some wooden supports on the ice before putting the plate of strawberries on top. Then cover the container with a towel.

The ice sublimes and CO_2 displaces the air under the towel. After lying in the CO_2 atmosphere for 30 minutes, the strawberries will have absorbed the gas. When you eat them, the CO_2 will dissolve on your tongue, creating bubbles and a sparkling sensation in your mouth.

2 Work with a partner. Discuss these questions.

1 Roughly how long does it take to make this dish?
2 What unusual property does dry ice have?
3 Why do the strawberries taste or feel unusual?

3 Underline these prepositions in the recipe. What kind of word follows them?

by	without	instead of	before	after

Preposition + -ing

When a verb follows a preposition, use the **-ing** form of the verb.
*Lay supports on the dry ice **before putting** the plate on top.*
*Instead of **melting**, CO_2 sublimes.*
NOT *before to put, instead of melt.*

4 Complete another recipe with the *-ing* form of these verbs.

stir	add	make	serve	wear

Strawberry ice cream

Entertain your dinner guests by ....[1] ice cream with liquid nitrogen (LN_2). First, put some milk, cream, and sugar in a bowl. After ....[2] to dissolve the sugar, mix in some strawberries. Then slowly add liquid nitrogen, stirring all the time. Don't do this without ....[3] gloves because liquid nitrogen can cause instant frostbite. Wait for all the LN_2 to sublime before ....[4]. (Instead of ....[5] strawberries, you can mix in coffee or pieces of chocolate if you prefer.)

5 Use the prepositions below to complete the sentences.

instead of   without   after   before   by

1 You can't make an omelette *without* cracking eggs.
2 Cover the turkey with aluminium foil .... putting it in the oven.
3 Melt the butter .... heating it gently in a pan.
4 If the fat is hot enough, the fish will fry .... absorbing it.
5 For a healthy alternative, use artificial sweeteners .... sugar.
6 The flesh of an apple turns brown .... being exposed to air.
7 You can slow this oxidization process down .... refrigerating the apple.
8 .... handling food, ensure your hands are spotlessly clean.
9 You can grate the cheese .... slicing it if you prefer.
10 I need a rest .... cooking all this food. Who's washing up?

6 How much do you know about science in the kitchen? Work in pairs or groups and discuss these questions.

1 Why do strands of spaghetti sometimes stick together when they're cooking? How can you avoid this?
2 Why does chopping onions make people's eyes water? How can you chop onions without crying?

7 Read the explanations and find out if you were correct.

1

When spaghetti is cooked in boiling water, a white cloudy substance is released. This is starch, a carbohydrate also found in potatoes, rice, and bread. Starch is a sticky substance which can make the strands of spaghetti adhere. You can't remove the starch, but you can dilute it by boiling the spaghetti in plenty of water. Adding oil to the water before cooking will have no effect because it will simply float on top.

2

It's difficult to chop onions without crying because they contain volatile sulphur compounds which change into gas very suddenly. The human eye responds by producing tears in order to dilute them. You can create a barrier by wearing goggles, but this will probably be inconvenient. You can oxidize the sulphur compounds by placing a lighted candle near the chopping board. Or you can stick your tongue out while you're chopping, so the compounds dissolve on your tongue before reaching your eyes.

8 Work in pairs.

1 Think of a local dish that a foreign visitor to your country might enjoy. Write a description of how it's made.
2 Read your description to the class without telling them the name of the dish. See if they can guess what it is.

Making conversation

1 Some people from another country are visiting your company and you're having lunch with them. Which of these conversation topics would you:

- like to talk about? (Why?)
- avoid? (Why?)

1 Where the visitors come from
2 Food
3 The work you're doing together
4 Religion
5 Sport
6 Movies
7 How much money you all earn
8 The weather
9 People you all know
10 Your previous jobs and careers
11 How old you are
12 Your families
13 Things you do in your free time
14 Politics
15 How much your cars cost
16 Holidays
17 The building you're in
18 Items in the news
19 Your health problems
20 Something else (What?)

In your opinion, which are the best three topics? (Why?)

2 Read some advice for making conversation. Which piece of advice is most important? Can you add any more suggestions?

THREE GOLDEN RULES FOR MAKING CONVERSATION FLOW

---

1 Smile and be positive.

2 Show you're interested. React to what people say and ask questions.

3 Listen. Everyone loves a good listener.

3 🎧 Listen to three conversations where people are making small talk.

1 What topics do they talk about?
2 Do they break any of the golden rules? If so, which ones?

4 Listen to the first conversation again. What could the man say to help the conversation along?

5 🎧 Listen to the second conversation again. What things does the woman say that show she isn't listening?

6 Listen to the third conversation again. How did the woman respond to these statements?

1 I had to work on the night shift last month.
2 I just got used to working nights and they put me back on the day shift.

7 🎧 Listen to another conversation. Why does this one flow better than the others?

8 🎧 Complete these sentences. Then listen and check your answers.

1 .... you .... have a factory in York Road?
2 It's a bit of a .... , but we're .... it.

9 Practise the expressions. Think of three things that:

1 you used to do in the past that you don't do anymore.
2 you weren't used to in the past that you later got used to.

10 Work with a partner. Take turns to read a statement and react with the comments below.

1 I'm afraid I can't come to Serge's farewell party on Friday.
2 My daughter had a baby on Thursday, so I'm a granddad now.
3 It's so frustrating to see that all our time and effort was wasted.
4 We're going to finish on time and on budget.
5 Ted was injured in a car crash last week.
6 The flight's been delayed by an hour.
7 This new material is 100 times stronger than steel.
8 The elevator's out of service and we live on the seventh floor.

a That's excellent news.
b Oh, that's a pity.
c That's a nuisance.
d Oh, no!
e Really? That's amazing.
f That must be difficult for you.
g Congratulations.
h Yes, I can imagine.

11 Work with a partner. Act out two conversations.

A – Use the information below.
B – Use the information in file 34 on page 101.

1 It's very crowded today in the staff canteen, but there's a free seat opposite **B**. Be sociable. Begin by asking, *Is this seat taken?* and try to develop a conversation. Follow the three golden rules of conversation in **2**.
2 You're sitting on a crowded train. It's very hot, you have a headache, and you're feeling very unsociable. You don't want to speak to anyone. **B** will try to make conversation with you but you should break the three golden rules.

12 Compare how the two conversations progressed. What happened when you broke the golden rules?

13 Play a game with a partner. Turn to file 9 on page 91.

Work in pairs. Put a counter on a start position and travel across the board. Use the phrases to begin and develop different conversations. Try to land on as many different colours as possible.

11 What do you think?

Making predictions

1 Read some predictions scientists have made about the future. Match each one to a topic.

1 New materials and inventions
2 Computers and artificial intelligence
3 The human body and medicine
4 The human mind
5 Creatures from space

2 Look at the words and phrases in italics in the text. Match each one to the correct definition.

1 artificial materials that have special properties because of their structure
2 something that gives a reason for believing something
3 important discovery or development
4 the smallest living parts of an animal
5 parts of the human body that have a particular function
6 the science of building devices from single atoms and molecules
7 put something in a particular place or position
8 removing people's body parts and putting them into other people's bodies
9 people who give part of their body for medical use
10 an experiment where a human judge engages in two conversations, one with a human and one with a machine. If the judge cannot tell which is which, then the machine will pass the trial.

Brave New World

As part of its 50th anniversary celebrations, the New Scientist magazine asked some of the world's most brilliant scientists for their predictions for the next 50 years. Here are some of the things they said:

How far will we get in 50 years? By then we will almost certainly have machines that can pass the *Turing Test* and communicate with us just as well as a human being.

– Terry Sejnowski, the Francis Crick Professor at the Salk Institute for Biological Studies

One exciting *breakthrough* in biomedicine will be the ability to produce human *organs* like kidneys and hearts for *transplants*. They will be grown by introducing human *cells* into animals, so we won't need human *donors*. But one organ we might not want to do this with is the brain. We probably won't want to put a human brain in an animal body.

– Bruce Lahn, Geneticist at the University of Chicago

Nanotechnology and *metamaterials* will revolutionize our lives. New materials and inventions are likely to be developed that no one has thought of yet.

– Nathan Myhrvold, Co-founder of Intellectual Ventures and formerly Chief Technology Officer at Microsoft

In the next 50 years we may find *evidence* of alien life in the frozen surface of Mars. We could also find alien life forms here on Earth.

– Chris McKay, Planetary Scientist at NASA Ames Research Center

We can already *plant* false memories into the minds of ordinary people – memories such as being lost in a shopping mall or cutting your hand on broken glass. Over the next 50 years we will probably become expert at planting more memories.

– Elizabeth Loftus, Psychologist working on human memory, University of California, Irvine

3 Work in pairs or groups. Discuss these questions.

1 Which predictions do you think will come true? (Why?)

2 Which predictions do you think will not come true? (Why?)

3 Which prediction would you most like to come true? (Why?)

4 Do any of the predictions worry you? (If so, why?)

4 Look at the text again. How sure are the scientists about their predictions? Find words and expressions that indicate they are not 100% certain.

5 Complete the diagram below with these words and expressions.

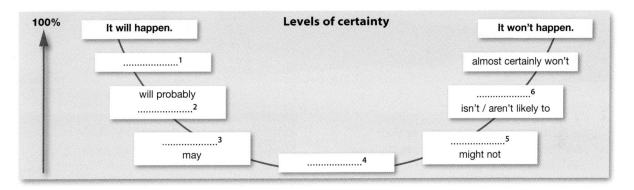

| may not | probably won't | might | will almost certainly | is / are likely to | could |

Levels of certainty

100%

It will happen.

....................¹

will probably ....²

....................³
may

....................⁴

It won't happen.

almost certainly won't

....................⁶
isn't / aren't likely to

....................⁵
might not

6 Read some more predictions. Do you think they will happen in the next 20 years? Insert expressions from the chart so they express your views. Compare your answers with some other students. Do you agree?

① We will all use flying cars.

② Robots will run our homes. They'll feed the cat, clean the kitchen, take out the rubbish, and check the kids' homework.

③ There will be a way to slow down the ageing process, and most people will live till they are 100 or more.

④ Prime numbers (indivisible numbers like 3, 17, and 23) are a mystery today. The higher you count, the more difficult it is to predict the next prime. But in 20 years we will understand their secrets.

⑤ There will be a crewed space mission to Mars. And in 50 years there will be a self-supporting colony on Mars. It will provide insurance against whatever catastrophes might occur on Earth.

⑥ We will develop drugs which can heal and regenerate our bodies and even 're-grow' lost fingers, arms, and legs. Complete body replacement will be routine.

⑦ Office software will be developed that has no bugs.

⑧ There will be revolutionary changes in city and town planning. People will live in village-like communities, not in suburbs far from their workplace.

⑨ Artificial intelligence will be very advanced and robots, not people, will make all the important scientific breakthroughs.

⑩ We'll have an inexhaustible source of safe, environmentally friendly energy.

⑪ We'll have more time to spend on our hobbies and with our families and friends.

⑫ We will discover that most of the predictions we made today are wrong.

Weighing alternatives

1 Have you ever been to a desert? Would you like to travel across a large desert like the Sahara? (Why / Why not?)

2 (18) Four people are travelling across the Australian outback. Listen to their conversation. What problem have they got and what are their alternatives?

3 Work with a partner. Answer these questions.

1 What exactly is wrong with their vehicle?
2 What alternatives do they have?
3 How far is the town?
4 How long could it take for a search party to find them?
5 What do you think they should do? (Why?)

4 Read a survival expert's opinion and find out if you were right. What will happen if they try to walk?

If they stay near the vehicle, their chances of survival are very good. With no water at all, people can survive for two days or more at temperatures of 50 °C. They need to find shelter and conserve energy. A very strong and experienced hiker might be able to walk 30 km a day if the ground is flat, but most people simply aren't fit enough. They will quickly become exhausted in the heat. Staying with your vehicle is the best alternative in nearly every case.

Gradable and ungradable adjectives

Some adjectives, like *tired*, *bad*, and *cold* are gradable. You can be *a little tired*, *fairly tired*, or *very tired*.
Other adjectives like *exhausted*, *terrible*, and *freezing* describe extreme conditions and are ungradable. We use more extreme words to modify them like *absolutely* or *really*.
Absolutely exhausted   *Really terrible*
NOT ~~Very exhausted / terrible~~

5 Look at the gradable adjectives in the sentences below. Suggest more extreme adjectives you could use in their place.

1 Our chances of survival are *very good* if we stay with the car.
2 We'll become *very tired* if we try to walk in this heat.
3 It's *very hot*.
4 The water container's *very big*. We can't carry it far.
5 I want something to eat. I'm *very hungry*.
6 There's so much dust. I'm *very dirty*.
7 The chances of someone driving by are *very small*.
8 It'll be *very cold* tonight.
9 But walking is a *very bad* idea.
10 I'll be *very angry* if they make me walk.

6 Match these ungradable adjectives to the correct phrases in **5**.

> freezing   tiny   excellent   furious   exhausted   boiling   enormous
> filthy   terrible   starving

7 Work with a partner. Act out a conversation using the sentences in **5**. **B** should
agree with **A** using an ungradable adjective.

>   **A** *Our chances of survival are very good.*
>   **B** *Yes, they're excellent.*

8 Read another survival problem and decide what to do. Should you stay where
you are or walk?

Your six-seater single engine plane has crash landed in northern Canada. The temperature is 15° below zero and it will get even colder tonight. There's snow on the ground and fir trees nearby. You think you're about 5 km off route from the flight plan you filed, and there's a small town about 25 km to the north-east. You're all wearing winter coats, hats, gloves, and shoes. Nobody is injured. You managed to rescue the following items from the plane:

	Extremely useful	Useful	Not very useful
A large knife	☐	☐	☐
An empty cigarette lighter (no fuel)	☐	☐	☐
One space blanket per person	☐	☐	☐
A compass	☐	☐	☐
A map	☐	☐	☐
A roll of aluminium foil	☐	☐	☐
A cosmetic mirror	☐	☐	☐
A loaded gun	☐	☐	☐
One pair of sunglasses per person	☐	☐	☐
A bottle of whiskey	☐	☐	☐
A large bag of jelly bean sweets	☐	☐	☐

9 Work in groups. Decide how useful the items are and compare your views with the
other students. Think of different things you can do to:

1 keep warm.
2 create a shelter from the wind and cold.
3 signal your position to rescuers.
4 stop yourselves from getting hungry and
  thirsty.
5 keep your spirits up.

10 🎧 (19) Listen to a survival expert discussing the
situation and check your answers.

12 *What's the problem?*

Handling complaints

1 (20) Listen to a call to a software company's help desk. What's the problem? Is the help-desk worker helpful? (Why / Why not?)

2 (20) Listen again and answer these questions.

1 What program is the customer trying to install?
2 What's his order reference number?
3 Did he type in the activation key?
4 What does the help-desk worker tell him to do?

3 Work with a partner. Read the listening script on page 114. Suggest ways the help-desk worker could be more helpful and polite.

4 (21) Listen to another version of the conversation. Does the help-desk worker do any of the things you suggested?

5 (21) Listen to the second version again. How did the help-desk worker sound more helpful? Make notes.

Explaining problems

The verbs *seem*, *appear*, *sound*, and *look* can make statements more tentative and polite.
The activation key doesn't work. → *The activation key doesn't **seem** to work.*
They are commonly used to give negative information politely.
*It **appears** to be faulty.*
*It **looks** like the system's a little slow today.*
*It **sounds** as if your antivirus program might be causing the problem.*

6 Make these complaints sound more polite. Use the words in brackets.

1 Three of the packages in the shipment aren't here (don't seem).
2 You're charging us too much (looks like / might be).
3 Your purchasing department lost our order (sounds as if / might have).
4 There are insufficient funds in your account (appear).
5 You put the wrong supplier number on your invoice (seem / have put).
6 We're not happy with the installation work. The wiring is loose (looks as if).
7 You underestimated the costs (appear / have underestimated).
8 You used the wrong kind of cartridges (sounds like / might have).

7 Match the complaints in **6** to the most appropriate response below.

a Yes, the figures we based them on might have been too low.

b What kind should I have used?

c I'll send an electrician round to look at it.

d That's not possible. I think the bank may have made a mistake.

e Oh, you're right. I'm very sorry. I'll send you a credit note.

f No, we've received it, but I'm afraid we're waiting for parts to come in.

g I'll contact the freight company and find out what's happened to them.

h Oh, I'm sorry about that. I'll correct it and send it again.

Practice making the complaints and responding with a partner.

Dealing with complaints

You can acknowledge a problem without admitting fault with *to hear that*.
I'm sorry to hear that.
An apology, explanation, and/or a promise to put things right is best practice.
Sorry to keep you waiting. The system seems to be a little slow today.
We'll sort it out now.

---

8 Think of a suitable explanation or promise to complete these apologies.

1 I'm terribly sorry I'm late …
2 I'm sorry I didn't call you back earlier …
3 I'm very sorry that we've billed you twice …
4 I'm afraid we won't be able to ship the parts until next week …
5 I'm afraid I can't attend the meeting on Friday …

9 Work in pairs.

A – Use the information below.
B – Use the information in file 18 on page 95.

A
You work in the purchasing department of a company that manufactures aeroplanes. **B** works in the sales department of one of your suppliers.
Your supplier is generally very reliable but there were a lot of problems with your last order. Call **B** and try to solve the problems. Use the notes below.

> You only received 70.
> 5 missing.

> Ext 1479 Hans Schuster.
> Your production team say they can't reach him on the phone and he hasn't replied to the email they sent him last Friday.

Order Form   ATR GmbH   15-18 Langenbachstr.   D-80799 München   +49-(089)-2867-0

Item No.	Description	Quantity	Unit Price	Total
TR16-957X	Wasp alloy blades	75	€415.00	€31,125.00
DD368-2B	Rotor discs	4	€3,675.00	€14,700.00
DB578-6B	Rotor discs	4	€4,756.00	€19,024.00
ST23-56R	Vanes	60	€356.00	€21,360.00
			Subtotal:	€86,209.00
			19% VAT:	€16379.71
			Total:	€102,588.71

OK.

Delivery address:
MTS Ltd
28 Grange Park
Patertown RH9 8TR
Kent
UK

> They shipped the wrong vanes!
> Correct vanes must be here by the end of the month at the latest.

> 1 disc needs to be re-worked. Should we ship it back or will they pay for the rework to be done here?

Describing damage

1 🎧 Listen to three conversations about some things that have gone wrong. For each one, make a note of what's been damaged or isn't working correctly.

2 🎧 Listen again and answer these questions.

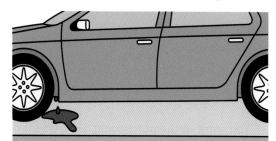

1 Why didn't Jack know the car was leaking brake fluid?

2 Why do the service technicians need to:
   a use ladders?
   b grease the joints of the tank?
3 What could be wrong with the filter?

go, get, and become

We often use *get* and *become* before adjectives to describe changes.
get dirty, become dirty   get twisted, become twisted
Get is more common than *become* in informal and spoken English.
We also use *go* to talk about changes for the worse.
The joints are going rusty. Something went wrong with the brakes.

3 Work in pairs or groups. Make a list of different things that can:

1 go rusty or get corroded.
2 get bent.
3 get dented.
4 get burnt or scorched.
5 get dirty.
6 get blocked or clogged.
7 go off, go stale, or go mouldy.
8 get cracked or broken.

4 Complete these sentences with a phrase from **3**.

1 Don't put coffee grinds down the sink. The drain could …
2 Use a larger knife to open that paint can. That little one could …
3 Carry those eggs carefully. I don't want any to …
4 Take off your boots. We don't want the carpet to …
5 We may need to store some of these medicines in the fridge so they don't …
6 Use a blowtorch to remove the paint, but make sure the window frame doesn't …
7 I'm always nervous when I'm parking in a tight spot. I don't want my new car to …
8 Don't leave the tools outside in the rain. They could …

5 Work in pairs or groups. Think of more expressions to describe damage and changes for the worse. Suggest suitable endings for these sentences.

1 Remember to turn the torch off when you've finished, so the batteries don't …
2 Please don't use these scissors to cut paper. I don't want them to …
3 If you leave your coat on the chair, it'll …
4 Learn to sew! Then you'll be able to mend your clothes if they …
5 Be careful with that red dye. You don't want your jacket to …
6 Lubricate the rollers so they don't …
7 Please cover the furniture before you start sanding the wall. I don't want it to …
8 Don't put the strawberries at the bottom of the shopping trolley. They could …
9 These CDs need to be put back in their cases. We don't want them to …
10 Don't put those porcelain cups in the dishwasher. I don't want them to …
11 Keep your passport somewhere safe. You don't want it to …
12 Wind those leads up and secure them before you put them in the box. Otherwise they'll …

6 Think of two or three things that could:

1 get lost or go missing.
2 go blunt.
3 get tangled.
4 get scratched.
5 get chipped.
6 go flat.*
7 get torn.
8 get crumpled or creased.
9 get dusty.
10 get stained.
11 get squashed.
12 get jammed.

a flat battery **BrE**   a dead battery **AmE**

7 A lot of things around our homes can get damaged if we don't take care. Look at the picture and find things that could get broken or damaged.

8 Work in pairs.

A – You have a beautiful home. **B** is looking after it for you while you're on holiday. They call you with some bad news. Find out what's happened.
B – Turn to file 43 on page 104.

Prepositions + *-ing*

1 We can use *by* + *-ing* and *without* + *-ing* to describe how to do something.

Examples
*Start the machine **by** pressing this button.*
*I loosened the seat **without** using a hammer.*

Use these ideas to make sentences with *by* or *without* + *-ing*.
1 He fixed the light. He replaced the bulb.
2 I built the cabinet. I didn't look at the manual.
3 They carried the piano up two flights of stairs. They didn't stop.
4 I guessed what was in the box. I shook it.
5 She managed to remove the cover. She didn't break it.
6 We got rid of the smell. We opened the windows.
7 I loosened the labels. I squirted them with Mr Fixit.

2 There are many other common English expressions where *-ing* follows a preposition. Think of a suitable ending for these sentences. Use an *-ing* form.

1 Thank you for …
2 I'm looking forward to …
3 A new restaurant's just opened at the corner. How about … ?
4 I think I'll take the train instead of …
5 When I'm really tired, I often feel like …
6 I'm not good at writing in French, but I'm really good at …
7 Our customers generally insist on …
8 I'm thinking of …

3 Compare your answers with a partner. Were any of them similar?

Damage

1 Read across, down, and diagonally. Find nineteen words for describing damage in the puzzle.

S	Q	U	A	S	H	E	D	F	X	X	X
C	C	L	O	G	G	E	D	X	L	X	X
R	R	O	X	X	B	E	N	T	X	A	S
A	U	B	R	O	K	E	N	X	L	D	T
T	S	X	X	C	H	I	P	P	E	D	A
C	T	X	A	T	H	X	Y	T	A	I	I
H	Y	R	N	X	X	E	N	O	K	R	N
E	C	R	E	A	S	E	D	R	I	T	E
D	U	S	T	Y	D	X	X	N	N	Y	D
B	C	O	R	R	O	D	E	D	G	X	X

2 What could <u>not</u> happen to these things? Cross out the phrase that does not fit.

1 **a map**   *get torn*   *get crumpled*   *get jammed*
2 **a nail**   *go flat*   *get bent*   *go rusty*
3 **a parcel**   *get squashed*   *get chipped*   *get lost*
4 **a shirt**   *get scorched*   *get corroded*   *get creased*
5 **a pipe**   *get dented*   *get blocked*   *go blunt*
6 **a filter**   *get clogged*   *go flat*   *get dusty*
7 **a key**   *get lost*   *get cracked*   *get bent*
8 **a shower curtain**   *go mouldy*   *go stale*   *get torn*

3 Look at the words you have crossed out in **2**. Think of two or three things that they could refer to.

Example
get cracked – a mirror or a cup could get cracked

4 What problem or damage could result if you:

1 don't notice the oil pressure warning light in your car is on?
2 forget to turn your headlights off when you leave your car?
3 leave food out of the fridge?
4 don't realize a water tank in the roof is leaking?
5 drop a metal knife or fork into a waste disposal unit?
6 press clothes with an iron that's too hot?
7 spill some coffee on your computer?

How does it work?

1 Work in pairs or groups. Choose four words at random from different coloured circles.

Example
glass   mobile   furniture   vibrating

mobile   multi-lingual
inexpensive   computerized
do-it-yourself   transparent   artificial
magnetic   over-sized   battery operated
artificial   nuclear powered   electric
virtual   online   edible

hand-crafted   vibrating
shrinking   expanding   temporary
edible   flying   collapsible   rotating
levitating   mechanized   musical
inflatable   invisible   changeable
waterproof

paper   foam   wooden
rubber   concrete   neon
metal   plastic   glass   silver   steel
wax   gold   cloth   polythene
ceramic

machine   appliance
instrument   equipment   vehicle
furniture   sound system   car   clothing
exercise equipment   decoration   house
tool   website   security device
safety device

2 Put them together to make the name of something.

Example
vibrating   glass   mobile   furniture

3 Try to imagine how the thing you've created works.

Example
It might be a massage chair which can be moved from room to room in a modern beauty salon.

Then pick four more words and try again.

13 *What have you done?*

Skills and experience

1 Have you ever done any volunteer work? If so, what did you do? Has anyone you know ever worked as a volunteer? What did they do?

2 Read about some volunteering jobs. Which ones would you be good and bad at? (Why?)

VOLUNTEERING MATCH

Find the volunteer job opportunity that's right for you.

Put your skills and experience to good use and help us make the world a better place.

Are you good at wood and metal work? A charity that teaches school children how to sail is restoring a 19th-century Scandinavian sail boat. Hands-on, practical help urgently needed.

Do you enjoy working in global teams? An international medical science foundation is looking for someone to set up a website where scientists can collect, compile, and share data on the spread of tropical diseases.

Rewarding work for creative volunteers. A charity for disabled motorists is looking for inventive engineers, mechanics, and designers to help convert vehicles, so people who use wheelchairs are able to drive.

Water supply and sanitation engineers needed to supervise projects delivering water to rural communities in central Africa. Highly satisfying work for volunteers with good troubleshooting and communication skills.

A home for senior citizens needs patient, friendly volunteers with basic computer networking skills to help with setting up a computer centre and providing training and support to its residents so they can send emails and access the internet.

An international disaster relief charity needs well organized, detail-oriented volunteers to manage inventory in its warehouses and organize the distribution of supplies to victims of floods, hurricanes, fires, and so on. When disaster strikes, we work 24/7.

Conservation scientists working on projects in remote regions of the Amazon jungle need biologists, chemists, meteorologists, and logisticians to join them in environmental projects and scientific research. Must be willing to work in primitive conditions.

3 Work with a partner. Choose two of the volunteer jobs and decide what qualities volunteers might need to enjoy them and do them well. Complete this table.

Job	Should be good at ...	Should be experienced in ...	Should be willing to ...	Other personal qualities
1 Restoring a sail boat	practical tasks	wood and metal work	work hard work in a team	interested in the history of sailing mustn't get sea sick
2				
3				

4 🎧 Listen to a candidate being interviewed for one of the jobs.

1 Which job is she interested in?
2 Do you think she would be good at it? (Why / Why not?)
3 What other jobs might she be good at? (Why?)

5 🎧 Listen again and say whether these statements are true (T) or false (F). Correct the ones that are wrong.

1 Emily has been a mechanic for three years.
2 She's a production planner.
3 She has a Portuguese boyfriend.
4 She worked for a TV crew in the Sahara for 4 years.
5 She is good at troubleshooting mechanical problems.
6 She's had a lot of experience in research.
7 She's been interested in saving rainforests since she was a child.

Present Perfect vs. Past Simple

We can use the Present Perfect or the Past Simple to talk about actions that have finished. It often depends on what kind of time expressions we use.
We generally use the Present Perfect with *time up to now* expressions.
For example *ever, never, yet, recently, since, already*
We generally don't use the Present Perfect with *finished time* expressions.
For example *ago, then, after that, when, last week, yesterday*

---

6 Work in pairs. Decide which tense is correct.

1 I (*have played / played*) chess when I was a student.
2 I passed the written test but (*haven't taken / didn't take*) the practical test yet.
3 How many training courses (*have you done / did you do*) since you started here?
4 He was a service technician, and then he (*has joined / joined*) the training department.
5 She (*has qualified / qualified*) as an engineer last year.
6 The first job I (*have had / had*) was at a small electronics company in Lyon.
7 Enrico (*has been / was*) in charge of maintenance for over ten years now.
8 She (*has studied / studied*) chemistry at Leeds University from 2003 to 2008.
9 How long (*have you had / did you have*) your current car?
10 Have you ever (*went / been*) to China?

7 A volunteer recruitment agency is conducting interviews for all the jobs in **2**. Take turns to be candidates and act out the interviews.

A – Look at file 15 on page 94.
B – Look at the information below.

B
You have decided to take a year off from your job to work on one of the projects on page 60.
1 Decide which job you'd like, but don't tell anyone. Keep it a secret.
2 Take a few minutes to prepare. Then answer the interviewer's questions. Lie if necessary, but try to ensure you sound like the perfect match for the job you want.

Reporting progress

1  A supervisor is checking how this project is progressing. Listen and find out what things have caused delays.

2 Read the supervisor's status report. It contains five factual errors. Find and correct them. Then listen again and check your answers.

Milton Road Project – Status update

I inspected the site this morning. All the cable is laid and the trenches were filled in.

Delays have been caused by the weekend's heavy snow. Traffic has been a problem, too. 'No parking' signs have been erected, but cars are still being left in the street. Also, a water main broke which still needs to be repaired.

This project is behind schedule, but the foreman knows it has to be completed by Thursday.

3 Use the phrases to complete the example sentences below.

has to be done	can't be extended
has been repaired	is being laid
have been caused	are being towed
should be filled in	away

Passives – continuous, perfect, and modal forms

Use the appropriate form of the verb *be* and the past participle to form passives.

Delays ....¹ *by the weekend's heavy rain.*
Cars ....² *all the time.*
The water main ....³ .
The cable ....⁴ .
The trenches ....⁵ *by now.*
The job ....⁶ *by Friday.*
The deadline ....⁷ .

4 Discuss the schedule of another construction project. It's Monday, week commencing 13th May.

1 What's being done now?
2 What's already been done?
3 What can't be done until the plumbing's done?
4 What has to happen before the windows and doors are installed?
5 What should be done by the end of this month?

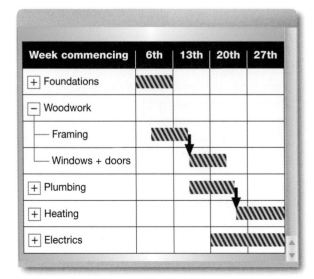

Week commencing	6th	13th	20th	27th
[+] Foundations	////			
[−] Woodwork				
— Framing		////		
— Windows + doors			////	
[+] Plumbing			////	
[+] Heating				////
[+] Electrics			////	////

5 Look at another project and say what's being done. What things could cause delays to a project like this?

6 Work with a partner.

A – You're the supervisor of the project in **5**. It should all be completed by next week. Ask **B** how it's progressing. Find out which jobs haven't been done yet and why.

B – You're the foreman of the project in **5**. Turn to file 13 on page 93.

7 Work with a partner. Think of a project you're involved in at work, at home, or at school. Take turns describing its progress.

1 What's the goal of the project?
2 What tasks must be performed?
3 What things have been done so far? (When were they done?)
4 What's being done now?
5 What hasn't been done yet?
6 Have any tasks been delayed? (Why?)

14 What's that exactly?

Technical writing

1 Read the text below and discuss these questions.

1 What technology is it describing?
2 Is anything unclear in the text? (Why?)
3 The text contains some mistakes. Can you find and correct them?
4 Can you suggest any other improvements to make to the text?

Roof surface spray cooling system

This new innovation in temperature control cools water during the night

water is sprayed over a building's roof and left to cool through evaporation and radiation. The coolled water is then collected, stored, and used to cool the building the the next day.

In tests, this fantastic system cooled up to two gallons of water per square foot of roof surface to temperatures well below the minimum night air temperature.

2 🔊 Listen to some people talking about the text and make the changes they discuss.

3 Complete the chart with the correct symbols.

Punctuation and capitalization	
?	question mark
	full stop*
	comma
	slash or forward slash
	hyphen
	brackets**
	apostrophe
	capital letters
	exclamation mark

*Am Eng: period   ** Am Eng: parentheses

4 Which punctuation should you use:

1 at the start of a sentence?
2 at the end of a question?
3 to separate items in a list or show where there is a slight pause in a sentence?
4 to enclose extra information within a sentence?
5 to join two words to form a new one?
6 to indicate alternatives or after *http* in website addresses?
7 after words or phrases that express strong emotion?
8 to indicate one or more letters are missing and before the letter s to indicate possession?

5 Read the rules for writers. Work in pairs. Correct the rules so they follow the advice.

Rules for writers

1 a sentence should begin with a capital letter and end with a full stop

2 Use commas to separate items in a list when you write letters emails reports PowerPoints manuals instructions and other documents

3 Don't use commas, which aren't necessary.

4 Don't use question marks inappropriately?

5 Never use multiple exclamation marks!!!!!

6 Its important to use apostrophe's correctly.

7 Only Proper Nouns should be capitalized.

8 BTW, remember not 2 use chat or TXT abbreviations.

9 Don't abbrev.

10 It's important to avoid colloquialisms, ain't it?

11 Check your speling.

12 Check to see if you any words out.

13 Verbs has to agree with their subjects.

14 Be carefully to use adjectives and adverbs correct.

15 Don't use no double negatives.

16 Roughly speaking, good technical writing is more or less specific.

17 Short sentences are generally best so avoid long sentences which go on and on because your readers will find it more difficult to know when one idea has stopped and another has begun and it will prevent you from getting your point across clearly and effectively.

6 Work in pairs to perform a 'running dictation'. It's a competition. You're going to dictate a text to one another. Read all the instructions before you start.

Instructions

1 **The preparation**
   A – Sit down and get a pen and paper ready, so you're ready to write.
   B – Keep this book open to this page and place it on a table or chair on the opposite side of the room. Then go and stand beside **A**.

2 **The dictation**
   B – When your teacher says *Go*, run to the other side of the room and read the beginning of the text below. Remember as much of the text as you can. Then run back to **A** and start dictating it.
   A – Write down what **B** tells you. Then give **B** the pen.
   A and **B** – Change places.
   A – Run to the other side of the room. Read and remember some more of the text. Then run back and dictate to **B**.
   A and **B** – Continue in this way until you have written the whole text.

3 **The quality control**
   When you think you have finished, show your teacher what you have written. They will check it for errors.
   The first pair to finish are the winners, but remember the text must be 100% correct. There must be no grammar, spelling, or punctuation errors.

Writing technical documents

The key to success in technical writing is to present relevant information in a logical way. This means your writing must be well structured. It's also important to KISS – Keep It Short and Simple. Short sentences and simple expressions make documents clear and easy to read.

A good writer adapts to their readers. So the words you use when you're writing for engineers will be different from the words you use with laypeople. Every professional field has its own specialist terms or jargon. Your readers must understand the terms you use, and if you think they might not know them, you should explain them.

'A picture is worth a thousand words' is a cliché, but it's true. The use of diagrams, charts, and flow charts can make technical ideas much easier to understand.

And finally, don't forget to use your computer's spelling and grammar checker. It only takes a few moments to set it up to work in other languages, and it's one of the most useful tools a writer has.

Measurements and conversions

1 What do you know about the metric measurement system? Work with a partner and discuss these questions.

1 In which country was the metric system developed: The USA, France, or Greece?
2 How did people decide how long a metre should be?
3 How big is a decimetre: 1/10 of a metre or 10 metres?
4 What's another definition of the volume of a cubic decimetre?

5 How much does a litre of water weigh? And how much do a thousand litres of water weigh?
6 Which countries don't use the metric system of measurements?
7 How many non-metric units of measurement can you name?

2 Read this article and check your answers.

Measuring the world

Back in the eighteenth century, French scientists wanted to create an ideal system of measurement. To ensure that measurement units would remain the same from place to place, they looked for constants in nature to form the basis of a new system. At that time they believed the circumference of the earth never changed, so they based the unit of length on the earth's polar quadrant. The distance from the equator to the pole was calculated and divided by ten million. That measurement became the metre, the foundation of the metric system.

Multiples of ten are core to the metric system. A thousand metres is a kilometre and on a descending scale, a tenth of a metre is a decimetre, a hundredth is a centimetre, and a thousandth is a millimetre. The litre was defined as a volume equal to a cubic decimetre and weights were also derived from natural constants. One kilogram was the mass of one litre of water at its melting point. So a thousand litres of water at zero degrees Celsius weighs 1,000 kg, or one metric tonne.

The International System of Units is the modern form of the metric system and its units of measurement are used in science and business around the world. The USA, however, is a significant exception. Non-metric (imperial) measurements that date back historically to connections with Britain are still widely used. So the weather forecast tells you the temperature in degrees Fahrenheit and people generally think in terms of old measurements like ounces and yards.

In the UK, metric measurement now dominates, but there are still areas of life where people use old imperial measurements. So someone might describe their height in terms of feet and inches, or their weight in terms of stones and pounds. They might talk about the fuel consumption of their cars in terms of miles per gallon, and in British pubs, people still buy their beer in pints.

3 Answer these questions.

1 What fraction of the earth's polar quadrant is a metre?
2 What number do you have to multiply a metre by to get a kilometre?
3 What number do you have to divide a metre by to get a decimetre?
4 How many examples of imperial measurements can you find in the article?

4 Use these words and phrases to complete the chart:

| minus | take away | times | works | roughly | plus | divided by | multiplied by |

Formal	Less Formal
3 + 2 = 5	
Three ....¹ two equals / is five.	Three and two is / are five.
6 – 2 = 4	
Six ....² two equals / is four.	Six ....³ two leaves / is four. Two from six leaves / is four.
3 x 5 = 15	
Three ....⁴ five equals / is fifteen.	Three ....⁵ five is fifteen. Three fives are fifteen.
8 ÷ 2 = 4 $^8/_2$ $\frac{8}{2}$	
Eight ....⁶ two equals / is four. Eight over two.	Two into eight is / makes four.

Saying results and approximations	
That ....⁷ out to … That's exactly …	It's somewhere around… It's ....⁸ …

5 (26) Listen to some people converting metric measurements to imperial measurements. Complete the information about this gauge.

Part No.: 624550027L3

Materials: ....¹

Maximum Operating Pressure:
.........² bar ....³ PSI

Maximum Operating Temperature:
.... ⁴ °C .... ⁵ °F

Price: ....⁶

Discount rate: ....⁷

6 (26) Listen again and write the calculations they make to:

a convert bar to PSI.
b convert from Celsius to Fahrenheit.
c work out the discounted price.

7 Follow these instructions and write down a calculation. What does it work out to?

> Think of a number and write it down. Multiply it by 2 and add 2. Multiply the result by 3 and add 3. Take away the original number and then subtract 9 from the result.
> Divide by 5 and you should be back to the original number.

Use the phrases from exercise 4 to say your calculation aloud.

8 Write down a simple sum using any combination of these symbols: + – ÷ x =

Dictate your sum to the class but don't give the result. They should tell you the answer.

Describing location

1 This site plan is incomplete. Use the information below to label all the buildings.

1 The body shop is located between the paint shop and the press shop.
2 There's a multi-storey car park opposite the gatehouse.
3 The gym is next to the canteen.
4 The warehouse is near the assembly shop. It backs onto the railway tracks.
5 There's a roundabout in front of the administration building.
6 If you're facing west, the R&D building is behind the maintenance building.
7 The foundry is located on the northern boundary of the site, behind the machine shop.

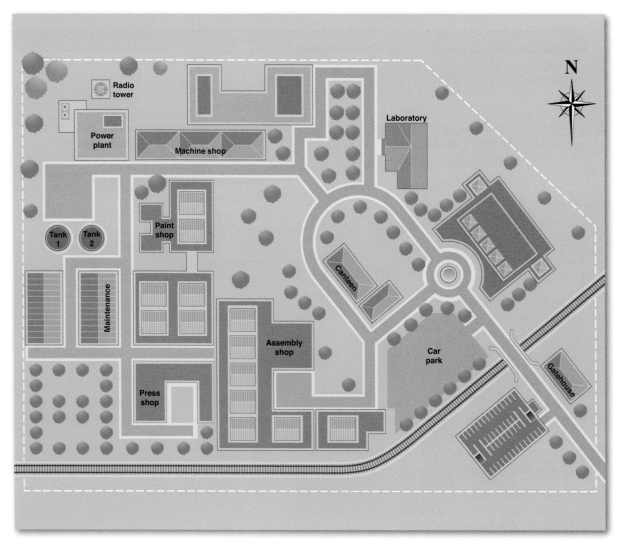

2 Here's some more information about the site, but it's wrong. Correct it.

1 The maintenance building is opposite the paint shop.
2 The paint shop is next to the press shop.
3 The R&D building is near the administration building.
4 There's a radio tower in front of the power plant.
5 The lab is located in the south-west corner of the site.
6 You go under a railway track to enter the site.
7 The railway track runs between the warehouse and the assembly shop.

3 (27) The site plan shows the buildings, but it doesn't show utility lines, such as sewers, water pipes, electricity cables, and so on. Listen to someone talking about tracing a sewer line on the site. Mark where it runs.

4 (27) Listen again and answer these questions about the different sections of the pipe.

1 What different materials is the pipe made of? Mark them on the site plan.
2 How did they trace its different sections?

5 (27) Listen again and complete the sentences.

1 It was quite a job to .... the main sewer line, but we now know where it ....
2 It was pretty easy to see where it .... direction. At the gatehouse it .... south-west, and then west.
3 It .... to the railway track .... it .... to a .... roughly .... with the south-west corner of the assembly shop.
4 We found the pipe suddenly .... north-east, ... the canteen and heading towards the lab.
5 But then it .... and heads north-west again. Just before it .... the paint shop, it becomes a clay pipe.
6 Then just .... tank 1 and 2, it turns north and .... the site.

6 Draw diagrams to illustrate these words and expressions.

Example

turns right	heads north-west	veers to the left	passes under
goes between	does a U-turn	runs parallel to	crosses

7 Work with another student. Compare your diagrams. Are they the same? Which are better? (Why?)

8 Work with a partner. Take turns describing the location of other buried utility lines on the site plan.

A
1 Draw a buried electricity cable on the site plan. It should start at the R&D building and after that it can go in any directions you like.
2 Describe where your cable goes, so **B** can draw it.

B
1 Draw a buried telecom cable on the site plan. It should start at the multi-storey car park and after that it can go in any directions you like.
2 Describe where your cable goes, so **A** can draw it.

Getting organized

1 What's your workspace like? Do you have your own desk or workbench? Is it generally clean and tidy? Describe it to another student.

2 Read about the principles of 5S. Have you ever applied principles like these to your workspace?

3 Look at the diagram and pictures and discuss these questions.

   1 In what different ways would companies benefit from applying 5S procedures?
   2 In what ways could you benefit from applying 5S procedures to your life outside work?

4 🔊 Listen to three conversations. Are they about *sorting*, *straightening*, or *sweeping and shining*?

The Principles of 5S

5S is a way of organizing and managing the workspace that originated in Japan. The idea is to follow a process so you're continually making changes that improve efficiency and productivity. The five steps in the process all begin with S, which is how it got its name.

The first three steps are concerned with improving workspace organization and cleanliness, and the final two steps are about maintaining the improvements. But many people think 5S is much more than a set of workplace procedures. They think it's a good philosophy for life.

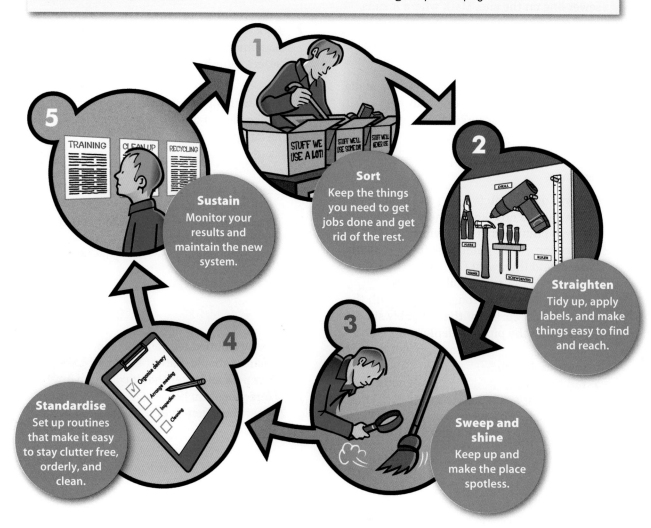

1 Sort Keep the things you need to get jobs done and get rid of the rest.

2 Straighten Tidy up, apply labels, and make things easy to find and reach.

3 Sweep and shine Keep up and make the place spotless.

4 Standardise Set up routines that make it easy to stay clutter free, orderly, and clean.

5 Sustain Monitor your results and maintain the new system.

5 (28) Listen to the first conversation again and answer these questions.

1 What exactly is the problem?
2 What will they ask maintenance to do?
3 Why does someone need to sweep up?

6 (28) Listen to the second conversation again. What do they decide to:

1 get rid of?
2 hold onto?
3 sort through?
4 get on with?

Which expression means:

a not let go?
b remove, throw away?
c continue doing something after an interruption?
d go through a number of things in order to tidy them or find something?

7 (28) Listen to the third conversation again and fill in the gaps.

1 I haven't .... putting it away.
2 I'll .... in a minute.
3 It's a little hard to ....
4 Then let's .... a simpler system.
5 Yes. I'll ....

What do the expressions mean? You can check your answers in file 20 on page 95.

Multi-part verbs

Many English verbs have two or more parts.
clean up   look for   come up with
Sometimes we can separate the parts and sometimes not.
Separable: *Clean up* the oil. *Clean* the oil *up*.
Inseparable: *Hold onto* those parts.   NOT ~~Hold those parts onto~~.
A good dictionary will tell you whether a verb is separable or not. You need to learn the verbs one by one.

---

8 Practise using some separable and inseparable verbs with a partner.

A – Read the list of things you want **B** to do.
B – Say you'll do them. Use *it* or *them* and separate the verbs if it's possible.

Example
A *You need to sweep up the store rooms.*
B *Yes, I'll sweep them up.*

A *And take care of the recycling.*
B *Yes, I'll take care of it.*

1 You need to *clean up* the work area.
2 *Put away* the ladders first.
3 Then *get rid of* the boxes.
4 But *hold onto* the plastic sheeting.
5 Just *work out* the best way to store it.
6 Then *tidy up* the store rooms.
7 *Sort through* the tool boxes.
8 *Throw away* any broken ones.
9 Then *check out* the oil pump unit.
10 There's a leak you need to *see to*.
11 *Figure out* what's causing it.
12 And you need to *get round to* painting the ceiling sometime.
13 So *look for* ways to work faster.
14 Well, I'll leave you to *get on with* the cleaning then.
15 Great. *Keep up* the good work!

9 Work in pairs or groups. Discuss ways you can improve your personal productivity by employing 5S principles.

1 Think of something in your life that you'd like to organize better. It could be:
a a place such as your car, your garage, or your office.
b how emails and files are stored on your computer.
c a task you do on a regular basis, like grocery shopping or studying English.

2 Interview one another about how you organize things at the moment. Can you come up with any improvements? Try to think of ways that you can employ 5S principles to do things better.

3 Share any good ideas you have with the class. Does anyone else have ideas you'd like to implement?

Converting measurements

1 Match these non-metric measurements to their metric equivalents.

1	1 mile	a	1 metric tonne
2	100 mph	b	11.7 L / 100 kilometres
3	3.94 inches	c	1.6 kilometres
4	2,205 lb	d	56.8 centilitres
5	10 feet	e	3.05 metres
6	0 °Fahrenheit	f	74.6 kW
7	20 mpg*	g	160 km/h
8	100 hp	h	100 mm
9	1 ounce	i	– 17.8 °Celsius
10	1 British pint	j	28 gm

*US gallons

2 Work in pairs or groups. Test your knowledge of international measuring systems with this quiz.

Measurement Quiz

1 If *m* is the symbol for metre in 1 m, should you write two metres as 2 ms?

2 Which spellings are correct: *metre* and *litre*, or *meter* and *liter*?

3 How about *grammes* and *grams*? Are they the same things?

4 Are tons and tonnes the same thing?

5 What's the difference in volume between a cubic centimetre (cm^3) and a millilitre (mL)?

6 How should you pronounce the word *kilometre*?

What's happened?

Play a memory game with the class.

1 Choose two students to play first. They look at the classroom and try to memorize the position of everything. Then they leave the room for a minute.

2 The rest of the class moves some things around or changes them.

3 When the students return, they should say what's been changed. For example: *The window's been opened. The whiteboard's been cleaned. The table's been moved.*

7 Is the symbol for litre *L* or *l*?

8 Does *K* stand for a thousand in computer related terms?

9 Do you say *Kelvins* or *degrees Kelvin*? And what's the difference between Celsius and Centigrade? Which one should you use?

10 How should you punctuate this large number: *150000000*?

Turn to file 24 on page 97 to check your answers.

Prepositions

What's the position of the black dot? Complete the spaces with these words.

below	on	on top of	near	on the bottom of	next to
in	in	in front of	behind	over	on

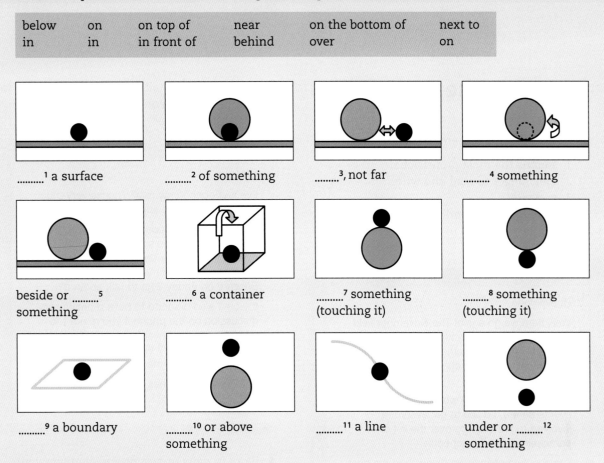

..........¹ a surface

..........² of something

..........³, not far

..........⁴ something

beside or ....⁵ something

..........⁶ a container

..........⁷ something (touching it)

..........⁸ something (touching it)

..........⁹ a boundary

..........¹⁰ or above something

..........¹¹ a line

under or ....¹² something

Have you ever ... ?

Work in pairs. Take turns to find out if your partner has ever done these things. If they have, ask more questions to find out more.

Example
have a second job (what kind)
A *Have you ever had a second job?*
B *Yes, I have.*
A *What kind of job was it?*
B *I drove a taxi in the evenings.*

1 break or damage something at work (what / how)
2 disagree with your boss (what about)
3 find an old friend via the internet (who)
4 forget an important appointment (what happened)
5 see your name in the company newsletter or another newspaper (why)
6 do an IT course (what kind)
7 work longer than 10 hours in one go (why)
8 lose a file or document (what kind)
9 send an important email to the wrong person (what happened)
10 fall asleep at your desk (when)

To be precise

Being concise

1 Compare these two emails. Which one:

1 sounds the most professional?
2 took longer to read and write?
3 is clearer?
4 sounds more friendly?
5 would you prefer to write or receive? (Why?)

> Hi everyone,
>
> Well, here we go again! The November field kick-off meeting is quickly approaching and it looks like we have another great programme. I'm attaching a draft schedule for you to have a look at.
>
> Even though we've all worked on these events before, I'd like to get everyone involved together to go over the list of participants and the schedule.
>
> I've checked everyone's diaries and the best date looks like next Wednesday, 18 March, from 12.30 to 1.30 p.m.
>
> Please let me know if you can come and I'll order sandwiches.
>
> Looking forward to working with you all on another successful event.
>
> Cheers,
>
> Eliane

> I'm attaching a draft schedule for the November field kick-off meeting. There will be a meeting for everyone involved on Wednesday 18 March, 12.30-1.30 pm. Please confirm you can attend.
>
> Eliane

2 Read another email. Can you delete words to reduce its length and still maintain a warm professional tone?

> Hi Yoko
>
> I've just opened my mail! Thanks very much for sending me the specifications.
>
> I don't know if it's possible, but it would be great to discuss the schedule when you're over in the UK later this month. Would you like to come to our main office in Leighton Buzzard on Friday 21st to talk about it?
>
> It would also be good to have a preliminary discussion on the phone if you're not too busy. Is there a convenient time for me to call you later this week? I'm free most days so please suggest a time that works for you.
>
> With very best wishes
>
> Stephen

3 Work in pairs or groups and compare your answers. Did you delete the same words?

4 Avoiding repetition is important for clarity. What words should be deleted from these sentences?

1 Please send us your flight details and please send us your hotel details.
2 Any information you can provide or give us would be appreciated.
3 I'll arrange a tour of our facilities, factory, and offices so you can see what we do.
4 We'd like to discuss and talk about the specifications with you.
5 I'm attaching some numbers and figures for the project in the attached file.
6 Don't hesitate to let me know if there's anything else I can do, and please tell me if I can help in any way.

5 (29) Two people are discussing an email they need to write about printed circuit boards. Listen. Make notes on what they want to say. Then work with a partner to write the email.

To:	john.warner@hjb-equip.net
Cc:	
Subject:	

Text abbreviations

1 Some people use text message abbreviations in their emails so they can be really brief. Match these abbreviations to their meanings.

1	4	a	today
2	U	b	excellent
3	R	c	for
4	2DAY	d	you
5	2MORO	e	no one
6	XLNT	f	are
7	NO1	g	tomorrow

2 It's probably a bad idea to use abbreviations like this in case they confuse your readers, but can you work out what they mean? Read this conversation with a partner.

A Happy bday 2 U
B THNQ
A WAN2 celebr8?
B I cant 2nite
A Y not? RUOK?
B Every1 is working L8
A OIC. Is NE1 looking at U?
B No. NO1.
A Get outta there B4 any1 CS U leave
B OK
A GR8 C U L8R

3 Work in pairs or groups. Write a text message to another group using some of the abbreviations. See if they can understand it.

Identifying parts

1 Look at the diagram of a four-stroke engine. What parts can you name?

2 Read descriptions of the different parts and label the diagram.

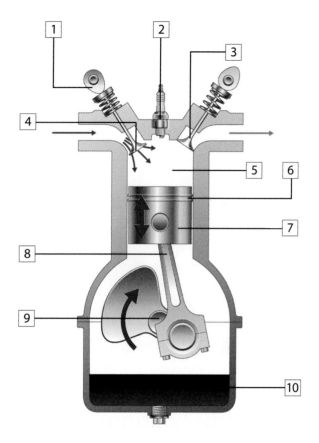

> **Piston** A cylindrical piece of metal that fits tightly inside a cylinder and moves up and down.
>
> **Combustion chamber** The part of an engine where fuel is burned.
>
> **Spark plug** An electrical device on top of the engine that creates a spark which ignites the mixture of air and fuel in the combustion chamber.
>
> **Intake valve** A mechanical device that controls the flow of air and fuel entering the combustion chamber.
>
> **Exhaust valve** Another valve which allows exhaust gases to escape.
>
> **Crankshaft** A rod or shaft with arms (called cranks) which stick out at right angles. Pushing the cranks rotates the shaft and converts the engine's power into movement.
>
> **Connecting rod** The part that attaches the piston to the crankshaft. It rotates at both ends so its angle changes as the piston moves and the crankshaft rotates.
>
> **Cam** A type of wheel with a bump on one side, used to convert a circular motion into up and down motion.
>
> **Sump** The lowest part of the engine lubrication system which has a plug for draining off the oil.
>
> **Piston rings** Sliding seals located between the outer edge of the piston and the inner edge of the cylinder which prevent the fuel-air mixture and exhaust from leaking into the sump. They also prevent oil in the sump from leaking into the combustion chamber.

3 Look at the descriptions again. What were the key words and phrases that helped you to identify the parts?

Identifying parts

There are many ways to identify parts and devices. Here are some important ones:

The class they belong to	*a device, a part, a type of wheel, a piece of metal*
Adjectives	*long, rotating, electrical, mechanical, cylindrical, sliding*
Components or features	*has a plug, with a bump on one side*
Locations or connections	*is located between, connects, attaches, fits tightly inside*
What things do	*creates, moves up and down, rotates, allows, prevents*
Purpose	*for draining off the oil, used to convert circular motion into up and down motion*

4 Work with a partner. Read some more descriptions. Identify and label the correct part or device below.

Nozzle A narrow part that's attached to the end of a pipe or tube that's used to direct a stream of liquid, air, or gas passing through.

Compass An instrument with a needle that always points to the north.

Hook A curved piece of metal or plastic for catching things or hanging things on.

Plunger A flexible rubber cup that has a handle.

Sprocket A wheel with a row of teeth around the edge that connect with the holes of a chain or holes in film in order to turn it.

Washer A small flat ring made of rubber, metal, or plastic that is placed under a nut. It reduces wear from friction between two surfaces.

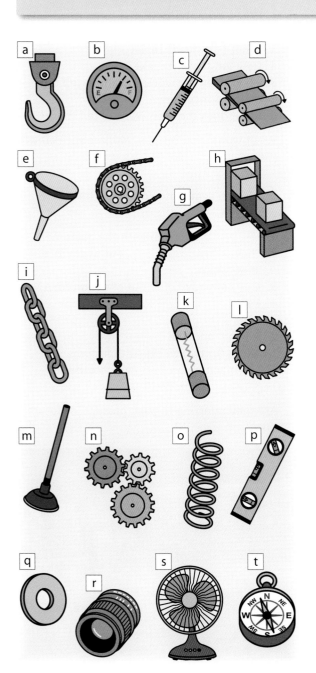

5 Use words from the list to label the other parts and devices in **4**.

gears	chain	conveyor belt	spirit level
syringe	fuse	rollers	lens
pulley	spring	funnel	blade
fan	gauge		

6 Work with a partner and check your answers.

1 **A** turns to file 21 on page 96 and reads descriptions of parts and devices. **B** listens and identifies the correct picture.
2 **B** turns to file 5 on page 89 and reads descriptions of parts and devices. **A** listens and identifies the correct picture.

7 Work with a partner. Write similar descriptions for these devices.

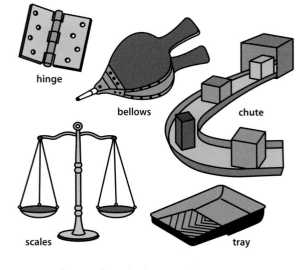

hinge

bellows

chute

scales

tray

Read your descriptions to the class. Which were the clearest? (Why?)

Organizing schedules

1 Read a story about a delay in a schedule. The events are in the wrong order. Number the events in the order you think they happened. (There are several possibilities.)

a	....	One of the supplier's production machines broke down.
b	....	When the part arrived, they repaired the machine.
c	....	A customer placed an order with a supplier.
d	....	The supplier called the customer and explained there would be a delay.
e	....	The maintenance crew discovered the machine needed a new part and ordered it.
f	....	The customer agreed to wait a little longer.

2 (30) Listen to the suppliers discussing the problem and find out if you were right. Which event in **1** hasn't happened yet?

3 Work with a partner and answer these questions.

1 When does the customer need their order?
2 When did the machine break down?
3 What part needs replacing?
4 How long could it take?
5 What does the woman want to tell the maintenance crew?
6 What does the man want to tell them?

What would you tell the maintenance crew? (Why?)

4 (30) Listen again and complete these sentences.

1 .... spoken with the customer.
2 They .... out of stock in three weeks.
3 .... already .... out of action for a week.
4 A ring .... loose and it .... the rotor.
5 But the machine .... out of action for two weeks at that point.
6 The machine broke down because it .... properly.

Are they referring to past, present, or future time?

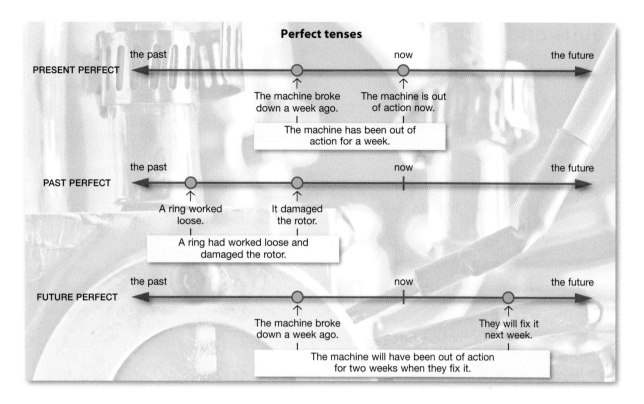

Perfect tenses

PRESENT PERFECT

the past — now — the future

The machine broke down a week ago.
The machine is out of action now.

The machine has been out of action for a week.

PAST PERFECT

the past — now — the future

A ring worked loose.
It damaged the rotor.

A ring had worked loose and damaged the rotor.

FUTURE PERFECT

the past — now — the future

The machine broke down a week ago.
They will fix it next week.

The machine will have been out of action for two weeks when they fix it.

5 Perfect tenses link two times. Which perfect tense links:

1 the past and the future?
2 the present and the past?
3 two past times?

6 Make some Past Perfect sentences. Match each beginning to a suitable ending.

1 After we'd finished carrying all the boxes upstairs,
2 Alf had worked in the assembly shop for twelve years
3 The bicycle had been left outside in the rain
4 The engine seized up
5 Nobody came to the web conference
6 I clicked 'send' and then I realized

a before he got a job in planning.
b I'd copied the whole company.
c because it hadn't been serviced for months.
d Harry offered to come and help us.
e so it was all rusty.
f because we'd forgotten to email the invitations.

7 Study the sentences in **6**.

1 All these things happened in the past, but which things happened first and which things happened later?
2 What tense do we use for the things that happened first?
3 What tense do we use for the things that happened later?

8 Practise making some Future Perfect sentences.

1 Make a list of some of the things you have to do in the next month.
2 In one week's time, how far along will you be? Say what things you will and won't have done.
   I will have … I won't have …

9 Work with a partner. You and your partner are presenting a project proposal to management next Friday.

A – Use the information in file 28 on page 99.
B – Use the information in file 36 on page 102.

10 Did you manage to organize your schedules? What had your partner forgotten to do?

Faults and hazards

1 Work in pairs or groups and discuss these questions.

1 Have you ever had to complain about substandard work that was done on your home or car? What happened?
2 Think of a product you've bought that has been faulty. Did you have to return it to the store or supplier? What happened?

2 Read some warnings about faulty products and match them to the correct picture.

1 This toy contains parts which could become detached and which may present a *choking* hazard to young children.
2 There has been *evidence* that the petrol tank may leak, *posing* a fire risk.
3 In certain circumstances these products may have an *intermittent* electrical fault, which could delay the alarm sounding in the event of an emergency.
4 These items may contain lead paint, which is toxic if *ingested* by young children and could cause *adverse* health effects.
5 In a small number of cases, this product is not up to normal quality standards and could *shatter* when being screwed into a fitting.
6 A *short* can cause the battery to overheat and melt or *scorch* the plastic case.

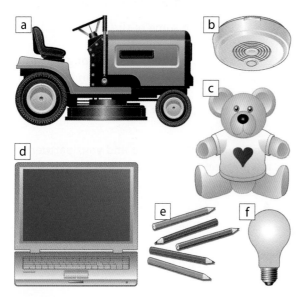

3 Look at the words in italics in the warnings. Match each one to the correct definition.

1 eaten or swallowed
2 burn slightly so its colour changes (but it's not destroyed)
3 stopping for a while then starting again
4 creating (a hazard or problem that needs to be dealt with)
5 being unable to breathe because something is blocking the passage to the lungs
6 negative, unpleasant, unfavourable
7 break into very small pieces
8 proof that something is true
9 have a failure in an electrical circuit

4 Have you ever bought a faulty product that was later recalled by the manufacturer? What cases do you know where this has happened?

5 Read a product-recall announcement.

1 What problems could the switches cause?
2 What might have caused the problem with the switches?
3 If you have one of these switches, what do you need to do?

Recall notice: Electronic motion switches – model KNJV40

We have become aware of a potential problem that may affect some KNJV40 switches supplied since April 2008.

The problem has arisen because some of the screws on the mounting block may not have been tightened sufficiently. This can cause excessive heat, which could lead to scorching, and in some cases the melting of the block and surrounding area.

If you believe that one of these switches might have been installed on your premises, please stop using it immediately and contact us immediately. Call Shallybank Electrical on 01379 555 780 or email krivers@shallybank.co.uk.

We apologize for any inconvenience this may cause.

Edward Howard

CEO, Shallybank Electrical Ltd.

---

6 Find these phrases in the notice. Are they describing past, present, or future possibilities?

may affect	may not have been
can cause	might have been
could lead to	may cause

Speculating

Present and future possibilities

The situation	may	be serious.
The heat	could	cause scorching.
It	might	result in the block melting.

Past possibilities

The problem	may	have been caused by the screws.
The screws	may not	have been tightened.

7 Read these situations with a partner and practise making past and future speculations. Say what might have caused these things to happen and what the results might be.

Example
Laying off 30% of the workforce –
We could have lost a major customer.
Our sales may fall substantially next year.

1 Your company plans to lay off 30% of its workforce next year.
2 There's been no public transport for the last week.
3 The building you work in was destroyed by fire at the weekend.
4 The population is ageing.
5 The government is rationing water.
6 Steel prices have increased by about 50% in the last two years.
7 You haven't been able to sleep at night.
8 You've discovered there's no money in your bank account.

8 Play a speculating game with the class.

1 Everyone should tear a piece of paper into eight pieces and have a pencil or pen ready.
2 Appoint one student as your leader. They read the problems below to the class, one by one.
3 After listening to each problem, everyone takes a piece of paper and writes down one sentence. It must speculate about one of the following:
   a A possible cause.
      It could / may / might be …
   b A possible result.
      It could / may / might result in …
   c A possible past cause.
      It could / may / might have been caused by …
4 Mix up all the sentences and redistribute them. Everyone should have a pile of eight sentences.
5 The leader reads the problems again, and each person reads the top sentence in their pile. Do they make sense or do they sound crazy?
6 Mix up all the sentences again and match them to the correct problem.

Problems
1 Your vacuum cleaner is making a strange rattling sound.
2 The air pressure in one of your front tyres is low.
3 There's a small puddle of water on the floor in front of the fridge.
4 The doctor took your blood pressure and found it was very high.
5 Your computer's antivirus program has stopped working.
6 A big crack has appeared in the ceiling directly above your desk.
7 You've received a large bill from a credit card company for items you didn't buy.
8 The waistband of your trousers seems rather tight.

Security

1 Read the laboratory security policies. Are there any areas or rooms in your place of work where similar policies apply?

> ### Research Laboratory Security
>
> **1** Doors should be locked at all times.
>
> **2** Cameras and mobile phones should be handed in to security before entry.
>
> **3** Any outside contractors entering the lab should be accompanied by security guards at all times.
>
> **4** Prototypes should be covered with a sheet when outside contractors are present.

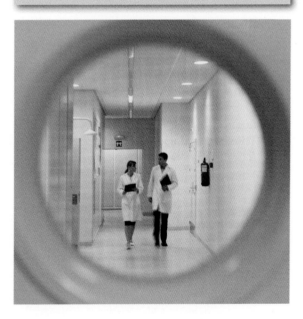

2 🎧 (31) Listen to some people talking about a security breach at the laboratory. What happened? Which of the four policies were breached?

3 Work with a partner. Answer these questions.

1 What photos have appeared on the web?
2 Who is very angry?
3 How many outside contractors were working in the lab?
4 What were they doing?
5 What's the head of security going to do?
6 Why did the men uncover the prototype?

4 🎧 (31) Listen again and complete the sentences.

1 I thought it .... top secret.
2 .... hand in cameras and mobile phones before they go in there.
3 They .... accompanied by a security guard.
4 I know, but we ....

> ### Should, be supposed to, and should(n't) have
>
> *Should* and *be supposed to* have similar meanings.
> We **should** hand in our phones. (It's the right thing to do.)
> We**'re supposed to** hand in our phones. (It's expected.)
>
> We use *was / were supposed to* when something didn't go according to plan in the past.
> *The contractors* **were supposed to** *hand in their phones, but they didn't.*
> (NOT ~~They should hand in their phones but they didn't.~~)
>
> We use *should(n't) have done* to talk about past events that didn't happen.
> *They* **should have been** *accompanied by a security guard.* (They weren't.)
> We **shouldn't have uncovered** the prototype. (We uncovered it and it was wrong.)

5 Work with some other students. Discuss security procedures you follow at work or school. Say what you *should / shouldn't* and *are / aren't supposed to do* concerning:

1 the security of the building you work in (access doors, ID cards, etc.).
2 your computer (locking it, passwords, shutting down at the end of the day, firewalls, anti-virus, mail encryption, etc.).
3 confidential information (classifying, clean desk policies, shredding, disposal of documents, etc.).

6 Work in pairs or groups. Read about some more security breaches. Say what *should have* and *shouldn't have* happened.

1 A confidential report about a new product was leaked to a competitor after an employee left it lying on their desk.
2 A service technician found copies of confidential documents in the photocopier when he was clearing a paper jam.
3 A visitor said she was late for an important meeting with the CEO. She was given a pass without showing ID.
4 A cleaner managed to access confidential data after they saw an employee typing his user name and password into his PC.
5 An employee didn't report a missing security pass. Someone else entered the building using it.
6 When a company connected its photocopiers to PCs, documents were printed at the same time as 'normal' photocopying was being done. Confidential documents were often thrown in the waste-paper bin.

7 Read a true story about some security breaches and answer these questions.

1 How did the strangers manage to enter the building?
2 Why were they able to get hold of financial data from the CFO's PC?
3 What did they find in the company's rubbish bins?
4 How did they get the CFO's network password?
5 Were the strangers criminals?

One morning, a group of strangers walked into a large shipping firm and walked out with access to the firm's entire corporate network. Here's how they did it.

They pretended to lose their key at the front door and someone let them in. Then they 'lost' their identity badges outside the secure area on the third floor and another friendly employee opened the door for them.

The strangers knew the CFO was out of town and they entered his office and took financial data off his unlocked computer. Then they dug through the corporate rubbish. They asked a cleaner for a bin, filled it with all kinds of useful documents, and carried it out of the building.

Next, one of them phoned the company, pretending to be the CFO (they had studied his voice). They said they were in a rush and desperately needed their network password. After that, they used simple hacking techniques and gained super-user access to the computer system.

In this case, the strangers were network consultants and they were performing a security audit for the CFO. The CFO never gave them any confidential information, but the company's security systems were so poor that they didn't need it.

8 Work in groups. Discuss these questions.

1 What shouldn't have happened here?
2 What should have been done to prevent this?
3 Could something like this ever happen in your school or workplace? What are people supposed to do that could prevent it?

Discussing risks

1 How effective are cyclists' helmets? Do they increase or decrease the risk of:

  a head injury?
  b being knocked down by motorists?

(32) Listen and find out what one researcher discovered.

2 (32) Discuss these questions with a partner. Then listen again to check your answers.

  1 Who is Dr Walker and what has he been researching?
  2 What's his most important finding?
  3 How did he discover this?
  4 Why is it a problem if motorists drive closer to cyclists?
  5 What experiment did he do with a wig?
  6 What did he discover?
  7 Does he normally wear a helmet?
  8 What are the odds of him being knocked off his bike on his way home?

3 Complete the expressions below with these phrases. Make sure the sentences are true.

less likely	more likely
are more likely to	no chance
the chances are	the odds

Likelihood expressions

Overtaking motorists ....[1] get closer if you're wearing a helmet.

Cyclists are ....[2] to get knocked down at a junction than anywhere else.

Dr Walker doesn't know if you're generally more or ....[3] to be knocked down if you wear a helmet.

If motorists think you're female, ...[4] they'll give you more room.

People disagree about whether a helmet reduces ....[5] of having a serious head injury.

There's ....[6] you'll be knocked off your bike if you go by car.

4 Work in pairs or groups. In your opinion, which of these events is more and less likely?

  1 Winning a jackpot in the lottery once in your life or being hit by lightning this year
  2 Dying from a shark attack or dying from contact with a poisonous animal
  3 Getting on a plane that has a drunken pilot or suffering a severe appendicitis attack
  4 Suffering from heartburn (pain caused from indigestion) today or having your identity stolen this year
  5 Dating a supermodel or having your marriage to a supermodel lasting for a lifetime

5 Work in pairs and find out if you were right.

  A – turn to file 32 on page 101.
  B – turn to file 26 on page 98.

Describing probability

The chances of winning the jackpot are 1 in 14 million.
The likelihood of winning the jackpot is 1 in 14 million.

*There's a one **in** three chance.* (33$\frac{1}{3}$% probability)
*There's a three **to** one chance.* (The odds are 3:1 – 75% probability)

We have special expressions for 50% probability.
There's a fifty-fifty chance. The odds are even.

We often talk about the odds against improbable things like this:
*The odds **against** being hit by a falling plane are 25 million to 1.*

6 Discuss this puzzle with some other students. Which answer do you think is correct? (Why?) What are your chances of winning?

You are taking part in a TV game show. The game show host shows you three doors. Two doors have a goat behind them and the other one has a car. To win the car, you have to choose the door with the car behind it, and you don't know which one that is.

You point to one of the three doors. The game show host doesn't tell you right away if you are correct or not. Instead, he opens one of the other two doors. This door has a goat behind it. Then he offers you a choice. You can stick with your original choice or switch to the other door. What should you do to maximize your chances of winning?

1 Stick with your first choice.
2 Switch to the other door.
3 It doesn't matter. The odds of winning are the same whatever you do.

7 Check your answer in file 37 on page 103.

8 Here's another game show puzzle. Discuss it and decide which answer you think is correct. What are your chances of winning?

This time you're competing in a two-player game to win the car. You and the other player both choose a door (not the same one).

The game show host opens the door your competitor chose and there is a goat behind it. They've lost! Hurrah! But can you win? You must still choose the correct door to get the car. The host offers you a chance to switch doors. Should you?

9 Check your answer in file 19 on page 95.

Speculating

1 Match each beginning to a suitable ending to make sentences.

1 A leak in the gas tank
2 The fire may have been caused by
3 Exposure to bright sunlight
4 A bug in the code
5 Loose screws could lead to
6 Salt in the atmosphere
7 An asteroid colliding with Earth 65 million years ago
8 The road accident

a could have been caused by poor visibility.
b might have caused the explosion.
c may have resulted in the extinction of the dinosaurs.
d may cause the steel bars to corrode.
e faulty wiring.
f excessive vibration.
g may have resulted in some numbers being rounded up rather than down.
h can cause the colour to fade.

2 Look at the sentences you've made. Are they speculating about the past or the future?

Project reviews

1 Here's a project that went wrong. What were the problems? What do you think caused them?

How the customer explained it

How the sales person described it

How the project leader understood it

How the analyst designed it

How the project was documented

How it was installed

How it was supported

How the customer was billed

What the customer really needed

2 Say what *should* and *shouldn't have* happened.

Examples
Someone should've found out what the customer really wanted.
The sales person shouldn't have promised so much.

Call my bluff

1 Read three definitions of the word *adze*. Only one definition is correct and the other two are false. Guess which one is correct.

1 If you need to cut or shape a large piece of wood, you need an adze. It's a heavy tool with a curved blade which is positioned at right angles to the handle. In American English it's spelt *adz*.

2 An adze is a special kind of pump that squeezes liquid along a hose. It has two or more rollers which squeeze the hose and force the liquid to move. The good thing about an adze is it prevents the liquid from coming into contact with the pump mechanism.

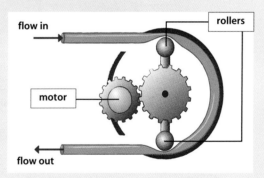

flow in   rollers

motor

flow out

3 An adze is a kind of gear which has a stick that works like a brake. The stick allows the gear to turn in one direction, but not the other. Adzes are often used for lifting equipment.

Check your answer in file 33 on page 101.

2 Play a similar game with the class. Form teams of three people. Each team should turn to a different file at the back of the book. See files 8, 11, 16, 23, 25, 29, and 41.

Safety or security?

1 Match the beginnings and endings.

1 Employees aren't supposed to enter
2 What am I supposed to do with
3 Aren't these plans supposed to be kept
4 Visitors should be accompanied
5 You're not supposed to give
6 You should shut down
7 You shouldn't leave documents

a all these old documents?
b in the safe?
c the building through the loading bay.
d containing sensitive information on your desk.
e your PC at the end of the day.
f colleagues your password.
g at all times.

2 Are these statements about safety, security, or both?

1 You're supposed to wear gloves when handling these parts.
2 You shouldn't have left it lying on your desk.
3 That door shouldn't be propped open.
4 You aren't supposed to work longer than 10 hours a day.
5 You weren't supposed to have told anyone about that.
6 You should have reported that incident earlier.
7 Those documents shouldn't have been put into the waste-paper bin.
8 These chemicals are supposed to be stored in a special cupboard.
9 You should wear this badge at all times.
10 You shouldn't have let him wander around the workshop on his own.

Information file

File 1

Unit 8, page 37

Causes and results, 6

Here are some ways to do the jobs better. Did you suggest the same things? Which solutions involve:

a training?
b redesign of the workspace, tools, or equipment?
c both?

File 2

Unit 2, page 11

Features and benefits, 9

B

1 Listen to your partner's description of an invention. What do you think the benefits could be?

2 Describe this doorway to your partner. Discuss what the benefits are.

FORM-FITTING DOORWAY

Motion detectors sense when a person or object is approaching.

Doorway opens just enough to match the shape of the person or object passing through.

3 Turn to file 17, page 94, to check your answers.

File 3

Unit 3, page 13

Giving instructions, 6

A

These instructions are in the wrong order. Number them in the correct order. Then explain them to your partner. Try to use some of these expressions.

Before you begin ...	First ...	Then ...
Next ...	After that ...	When ...
Once ...		

Painting a door

a .... Apply the undercoat and wait for it to dry.
b .... Fill any holes or dents.
c .... Sandpaper the surface to ensure it's flat.
d .... Apply the top coat.
e .... Wash the door down with water and detergent.

File 4

Unit 9, page 43

Inventions, 9

Describe this invention to your group so they can decide if they'd like to invest in developing it.

2 m x 40 cm ladder
Lightweight – weighs less than 1 kg – easy to carry around
Stable
No rattling noises
Rungs go only half way across
Strong, stylish

File 5

Unit 16, page 77

Identifying parts, 6

B

Read these descriptions to your partner and ask them to identify the part or device.

1 Cylindrical pieces of wood, metal, or plastic that roll over and over and are used in machines, for example, to make something flat. (Answer: rollers, picture d)
2 A curved piece of plastic or glass that makes things appear larger, smaller, or clearer when you look through it. (Answer: lens, picture r)
3 A device for lifting and lowering objects. It has a wheel or wheels and a length of string or chain. (Answer: pulley, picture j)
4 A metal coil that returns to its original shape after being pressed, pushed, or pulled. (Answer: spring, picture o)
5 A device that's wide at the top and narrow at the bottom, used for pouring liquids and powders into a small opening. (Answer: funnel, picture e)
6 A machine with blades that go round and create a current of air. (Answer: fan, picture s)
7 An instrument for measuring the level or amount of something. The level or amount is displayed by a needle and a scale. (Answer: gauge, picture b)

File 6

Unit 2, page 8
Specifications, 2

Here are the specifications of the Airboard Scooter:

Height	1200 mm (incl. handle)
Diameter	1600 mm
Maximum speed	25 km/h
Stopping distance	6 m
Maximum load	100 kg
Operating time	1 hour on a full tank of fuel
Construction materials	fibreglass / high-impact plastic shell / aluminium frame / rubber skirt
Engine	4-stroke Briggs & Stratton
Fuel tank capacity	5 L
Fuel	85 Octane unleaded
Approximate shipping weight	150 kg
Approximate shipping packing size	800 mm H x 1800 mm W x 1800 mm L
Colours	red, blue, green, and yellow
Delivery time	8–10 weeks
Price	$27,000

Are there any other statistics you'd like to know about this scooter?

File 7

Unit 9, page 43
Inventions, 9

Describe this invention to your group so they can decide if they'd like to invest in developing it.

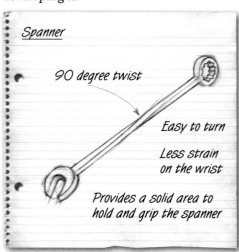

Spanner

90 degree twist

Easy to turn

Less strain on the wrist

Provides a solid area to hold and grip the spanner

File 8

Review and Remember 6, page 87
Call my bluff, 2

Here is the correct definition of the word *andiron*. Work together and write two false definitions. Read all three definitions to the class and see if they can guess which definition is correct.

If you have a fire at home, you may have an *Andiron*. An andiron is a support for wood in a fireplace. It's a horizontal metal bar where you put wood and burn it. Andirons have short legs and they are often attached to a guard that stops the wood from falling out of the fire.

File 9

Unit 10, page 49

Making conversation, 13

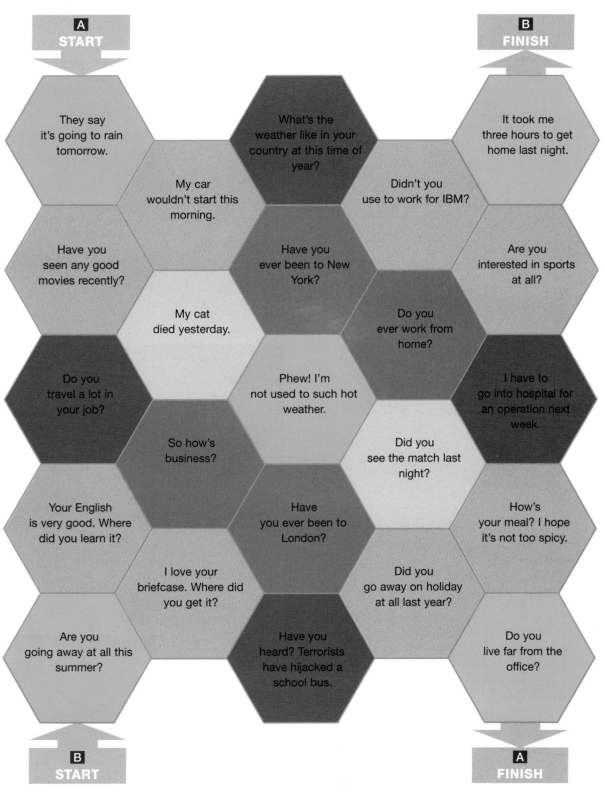

File 10

Unit 9, page 43

Inventions, 9

Describe this invention to your group so they can decide if they'd like to invest in developing it.

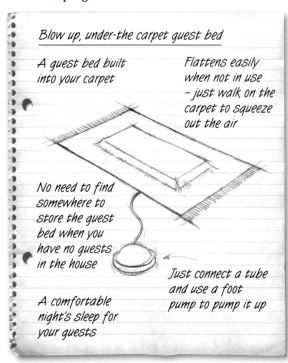

Blow up, under-the carpet guest bed

A guest bed built into your carpet

Flattens easily when not in use – just walk on the carpet to squeeze out the air

No need to find somewhere to store the guest bed when you have no guests in the house

Just connect a tube and use a foot pump to pump it up

A comfortable night's sleep for your guests

File 11

Review and Remember 6, page 87

Call my bluff, 2

Here is the correct definition of the word *crook*. Work together and write two false definitions. Read all three definitions to the class and see if they can guess which definition is correct.

A crook is a tool for catching sheep. It is a long wooden stick with a curved hook at one end. You can catch a sheep by placing the hook around its neck, or if you can't get close enough, round one of its legs.

File 12

Unit 7, page 35

Equipment documentation, 10

Here are pictures of the devices.

1 Are these inventions as you imagined them?
2 How do they work?
3 Do you think they could be useful?
4 Which do you like best? (Why?)

Hands-free umbrella head belt

Office equipment holder neck tie

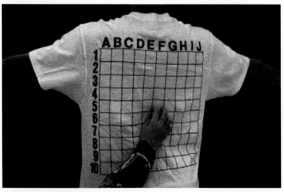

Back itch relief T-shirt

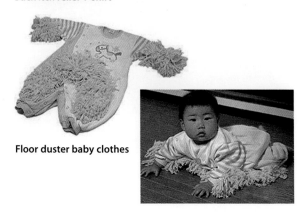

Floor duster baby clothes

File 13

Unit 13, page 63

Reporting progress, 6

Bad weather, sickness, late deliveries, accidents, and so on have caused
delays to this project. Tell your partner what has and hasn't been
completed yet.

File 14

Unit 9, page 43

Inventions, 9

Describe this invention to your group so they can decide if they'd like to invest in developing it.

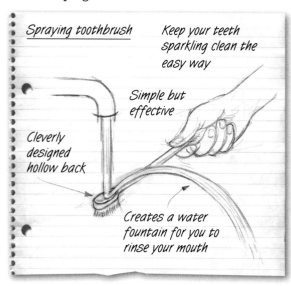

File 15

Unit 13, page 61

Skills and experience, 7

A

You are going to interview candidate **B**. Take a few minutes to prepare questions. Then do the interview.

1 Find out about the candidate's skills, qualifications, experience, and the personal qualities they could bring to the job.
2 Decide which job you think is most suitable for them.
3 Look at the jobs on page 60. Decide which one would be most suitable for the candidate.
4 Tell the candidate which job you think would be best and see if they agree.
5 Do you think the candidate was telling the truth or lying?

File 16

Review and Remember 6, page 87

Call my bluff, 2

Here is the correct definition of the word *flail*. Work together and write two false definitions. Read all three definitions to the class and see if they can guess which definition is correct.

A flail is a tool for knocking the hard shells off rice. It's made of two wooden sticks that are connected by a short chain. One stick is about 1.5 m long and the other stick is about 1 m long. The connecting chain is about 3 cm long. You hold the long stick and hit the rice.

File 17

Unit 2, page 11

Features and benefits, 9

How many benefits did you think of? Here are some possible answers.

The benefits of the Oliso™ Steam Iron:

The iron is more stable. It's less likely to get knocked over or fall off the ironing table.

It's safer. It prevents burns because the hot plate isn't exposed.

You don't have to lift the iron up, so you're less likely to get repetitive strain injuries.

The benefits of the Form-Fitting Doorway:

It saves energy and reduces your energy bills because you don't have to open the door all the way.

It helps maintain a stable temperature in a room.

It prevents dirt and other materials from being blown inside.

File 18

Unit 12, page 55
Handling complaints, 9

B

You work in the sales department of a company which supplies parts to the aero industry. You have recently moved to new premises and it has caused a lot of disruption to production.

A is an important customer, and they will call you with some complaints about their last order. (See below). Be polite and helpful. Provide excuses if necessary and try to put things right.

Order Form   ATR GmbH   15-18 Langenbachstr.   D-80799 München   +49-(089)-2867-0

Item No.	Description	Quantity	Unit Price	Total
TR16-957X	Wasp alloy blades	75	€415.00	€31,125.00
DD368-2B	Rotor discs	4	€3,675.00	€14,700.00
DB578-6B	Rotor discs	4	€4,756.00	€19,024.00
ST23-56R	Vanes	60	€356.00	€21,360.00
Delivery address:			Subtotal:	€86,209.00
MTS Ltd			19% VAT:	€16379.71
28 Grange Park			Total:	€102,588.71
Patertown RH9 8TR				
Kent				
UK				

File 19

Unit 18, page 85
Discussing risks, 9

Exercise 8 Answer: You should not switch to the other door.

If you switch, you'll only have a one in three chance of winning. Stick with your original choice and you will have a two in three chance of winning. Those are very good odds!

File 20

Unit 15, page 71
Getting organized, 7

1 This is what the expressions mean.

   1 get round to – find time to do something after a delay
   2 tidy up – make neat and orderly
   3 figure something out – understand, find an answer
   4 come up with – have an idea that solves a problem
   5 work something out – find a solution to a problem

2 Invent your own sentences using the expressions.

File 21

Unit 16, page 77

Identifying parts, 6

A

Read these descriptions to your partner and ask them to identify the correct part or device.

1 A set of wheels with tooth shaped parts on their edge that interconnect. (Answer: gear, picture h)
2 A series of metal rings which are linked together. (Answer: chain, picture i)
3 A long, continuous moving band of rubber, metal, or cloth, used to transport goods from one part of a building to another. (Answer: conveyor belt, picture h)
4 A glass tube partially filled with liquid which has a bubble of air inside. It's used for checking things are horizontal. (Answer: spirit level, picture p)

5 A plastic or glass tube with a long hollow needle or hollow rubber part at the end that's used for sucking up liquid and then pushing it out. (Answer: syringe, picture c)
6 The flat part of a knife, tool, or machine which has a sharp edge or edges for cutting. (Answer: blade, picture b)
7 A small wire or device inside a piece of electrical equipment used to break the current if the flow of electricity is too strong. (Answer: fuse, picture k)

File 22

Unit 9, page 43

Inventions, 9

Describe this invention to your group so they can decide if they'd like to invest in developing it.

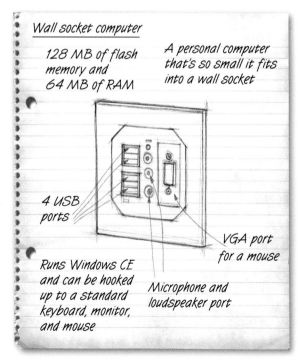

Wall socket computer

128 MB of flash memory and 64 MB of RAM

A personal computer that's so small it fits into a wall socket

4 USB ports

VGA port for a mouse

Runs Windows CE and can be hooked up to a standard keyboard, monitor, and mouse

Microphone and loudspeaker port

File 23

Review and Remember 6, page 87

Call my bluff, 2

Here is the correct definition of the word *chuck*. Work together and write two false definitions. Read all three definitions to the class and see if they can guess which definition is correct.

A chuck is part of a tool or machine that holds something tightly so it cannot move. Drills have chucks and they prevent the drill bit from moving out of place as it rotates.

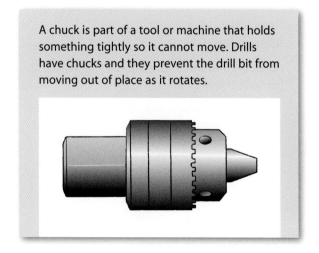

File 24

Review and Remember 5, page 72

Converting measurements, 2

1 The symbols for units of measurement don't have a plural form, so the correct symbol for two metres is 2 m (NOT 2 ms)

2 *Metre* and *litre*, and *meter* and *liter* are all correct. In British English, the *-re* spellings are used, while in American English, the *-er* spellings are most common.

3 *Grammes* are the same things as *grams*. The American English spelling is *gram* while British English uses both spellings.

4 Tons are complicated because there are several different kinds of ton. The three most common are:

   a the metric ton or tonne. 1 t = 1000 kg.

   b the short ton, which is generally just called a ton in the US. 1 ton = 2000 lb or about 907 kg.

   c the long ton, which was used in an old system of measurements in Britain called the imperial system. 1 ton = 2240 lb or about 1016 kg.

5 A cubic centimetre is exactly the same volume as a millilitre, so another abbreviation for cm^3 is mL.

6 People pronounce *kilometre* in lots of ways. In US English, the accent is usually on the second syllable, kiLOMetre, but in the British English it's usually on the first: KILLometer. Other measurement unit names are usually accented on the first syllable: MILLimetre, KILogram, MEGawatt.

7 Both L and l (with capital and lowercase letters) are correct symbols for litre. Most people prefer the uppercase version to avoid confusion with the number 1.

8 Theoretically *a kilobyte* should mean 1,000 bytes, but it actually means 1024 bytes (or two to the power of ten). *Megabyte* is another unclear term. Sometimes it means 1,048,576 bytes (a kilobyte squared), and sometimes means 1,000,000 bytes, and sometimes it means 1,024,000 bytes.

9 These days people say *Kelvins* rather than *degrees Kelvin*. *Centigrade* is an old term for *Celsius* and you should probably use the term *degrees Celsius*.

10 In English, commas are generally used to separate digits in long numbers. So for example: The speed of light in a vacuum is exactly 299,792,458 m/s. Decimals are marked by a point or dot. For example, the value of pi (π) is approximately 3.14159265. However, in some countries and languages, a comma is used to represent a decimal point. There is no universal international standard so you should use whatever is standard wherever you are.

File 25

Review and Remember 6, page 87
Call my bluff, 2

Here is the correct definition of the word *twist tie*. Work together and write two false definitions. Read all three definitions to the class and see if they can guess which definition is correct.

A twist tie is not something your boss wears. It's a thin metal wire covered by a thin strip of paper or plastic. It can be any colour and it's used to tie plastic bags. You put the twist tie around the top of a plastic bag and bend the wire.

File 26

Unit 18, page 84
Discussing risks, 5

B
Ask and answer questions about likelihood and complete the sentences. Use these question forms.

What are the chances of....?
What's the likelihood of...?
What are the odds of...?

1 The chances of winning a jackpot in the UK lottery are 1 in 13,983,815.
2 Your chances of being hit by lightning this year are about ....
3 The odds against dying from a shark attack are 300,000,000 to 1.
4 The odds against dying from contact with a poisonous animal like a snake are

  ....
5 The likelihood of being on a plane with a drunken pilot is 1 in 118.
6 The likelihood of suffering a severe appendicitis attack in your lifetime is

  ....
7 There's a 1 in 20 chance that your identity will be stolen this year.
8 There's a .... chance that you'll suffer from heartburn today.
9 The odds against dating a supermodel are 880,000 to 1.
10 The odds of your marriage to a supermodel lasting a lifetime are ....

Do any of the statistics surprise you?

File 27

Review and Remember 1, page 17
Size and distance, 2

B
Answer **A**'s questions and ask for the information you need to complete the sentences.

Example
How long is the Trans-Canada highway?

1 The English Channel is only 21 miles wide at its narrowest point.
2 The Trans-Canada highway is .... long.
3 Light travels at a speed of around 300,000 km/s.
4 Because of cosmic dust falling from space, the Earth's weight increases by about .... every day.
5 A human hair is strong enough to lift a weight of 2 kg.
6 The East Rand mine in South Africa is .... deep.
7 The Taipei 101 building in Taiwan is 508 m high.
8 A redwood tree can grow to a height of

  ....
9 The length of a day on Venus is 243 Earth days.
10 An Olympic swimming pool is .... deep.
11 The average weight of a male chimpanzee is 59 kilos.
12 The Blue Bridge in St Petersburg, Russia, is the widest bridge in the world. It's .... wide.

File 28

Unit 17, page 79

Organizing schedules, 9

A

1 Here's your schedule for next week. Before you present your proposal, you need to:

a update the budget with new cost estimates (3 hours).
b run some final prototype tests (4 hours).
c speak to the head of R&D (1 hour).

You can plan to do these things whenever you like. Write them in your schedule.

2 You also need to meet with your partner to rehearse your presentation. This will take at least 2 hours. Call your partner and schedule a time. Make sure they will have done these things before you meet.

a spoken to Marek Harlos in production planning
b prepared drawings of the prototype
c reviewed the project schedule
d kept Friday evening free so you can have a drink together

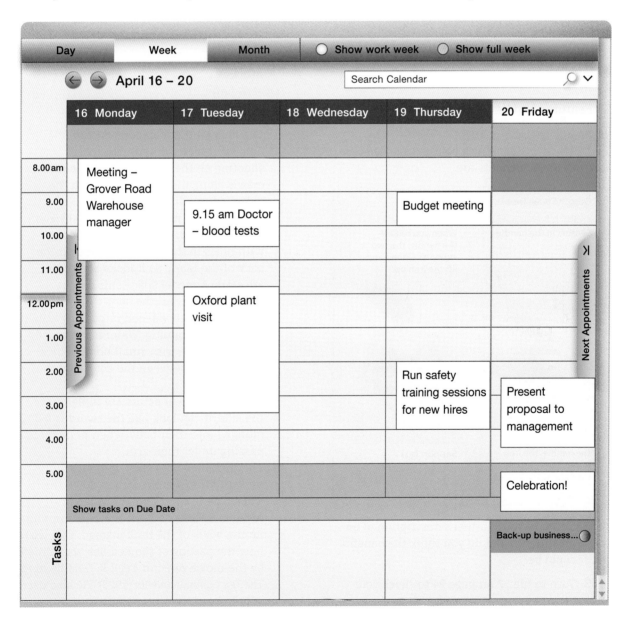

File 29

Review and Remember 6, page 87

Call my bluff, 2

Here is the correct definition of the word *thingamabob*. Work together and write two false definitions. Read all three definitions to the class and see if they can guess which definition is correct.

> If you forget the name of something, call it a thingamabob. People use the word *thingamabob* to talk about anything they don't know the name of. A thingamabob can be connected to anything, used for doing anything, and located anywhere.

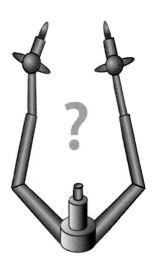

File 30

Unit 2, page 11

Features and benefits, 9

A

1 Describe this iron to your partner. Discuss what the benefits are.

Oliso™ Steam Iron

Sensors in the handle

When you release the handle, the two supports extend and lift the iron up.

When you touch the handle, the iron immediately lowers onto the work surface.

Support legs

2 Listen to your partner's description of an invention. What do you think the benefits could be?

3 Turn to file 17 on page 94 to check your answers.

File 31

Unit 4, page 21

Explaining processes, 6

1 The illusion that someone is climbing up a tall wall is sometimes created by shooting on the horizontal. So the actor crawls along the ground, but then the video is turned 90 degrees.

2 In low-budget movies, the night sky can be created with a piece of black fabric with holes in it. Lights are shone on the back of the fabric so it looks like there are stars. A model space ship can be transported across the shot with wires.

3 Actors are often videoed in pouring rain when it's not raining. Water is streamed through a tube with small holes, which is positioned between the actor and the camera.

4 In sword fights, if actors are filmed from the side, it can look like the sword is being plunged into their body, when in fact it is passing under their arm.

5 The trick here is to start with an empty tank and film water running down the sides. Then, if you play the video in reverse, it looks as if the water is running up the walls of the tank instead. This was how the parting of the Red Sea was filmed by the movie director Cecil B. DeMille in *The Ten Commandments* (1923). He also used jelly to keep the water apart.

File 32

Unit 18, page 84
Discussing risks, 5

A

Ask and answer questions about likelihood and complete the sentences. Use these question forms.

What are the chances of ... ?
What's the likelihood of ... ?
What are the odds of ... ?

1 The chances of winning a jackpot in the UK lottery are ....
2 Your chances of being hit by lightning this year are about 1 in 83,930.
3 The odds against dying from a shark attack are ....
4 The odds against dying from contact with a poisonous animal like a snake are 100,000 to 1.
5 The likelihood of being on a plane with a drunken pilot is ....
6 The likelihood of suffering a severe appendicitis attack in your lifetime is 1 in 700.
7 There's a .... chance that your identity will be stolen this year.
8 There's a 1 in 150 chance that you'll suffer from heartburn today.
9 The odds against dating a supermodel are ....
10 The odds of your marriage to a supermodel lasting a lifetime are 50:50.

Do any of the statistics surprise you?

File 33

Review and Remember 6, page 87
Call my bluff, 1

An adze is a tool for cutting and shaping wood.
Definition 2 describes a peristaltic pump.
Definition 3 describes a ratchet and pawl.

File 34

Unit 10, page 49
Making conversation, 11

B

1 It's very crowded today in the staff canteen, but there's a free seat opposite you. When **A** takes it, be sociable. Follow the three golden rules of conversation – smile, listen, and show interest. Try to develop a conversation.
2 You're on a crowded train. There's a free seat next to **A**. Follow the three golden rules of conversation again and try to develop a conversation. Begin by saying: *Phew! It's hot today, isn't it?*

File 35

Unit 6, page 29
Making comparisons, 6

Ranking (1 = most effective)

5 Switching to reusable cleaning products saves 5 kg of CO_2 a year.
4 Stopping buying new books saves a little more – 14 kg.
3 Using a push mower saves 36 kg, and you also keep fit.
2 Stopping junk mail saves 104 kg – the average adult gets 19 kg of junk mail per year.
1 Eating meat-free meals every other day saves 430 kg of CO_2 a year. It's one of the most useful things we can do. This is because of processing, packaging, transportation and also the natural gases animals produce when they digest food. Cows, sheep, and other livestock produce a lot of methane gas, which is even worse for global warming than CO_2.

File 36

Unit 17, page 79

Organizing schedules, 9

B

1 Here's your schedule for next week. Before you present your proposal to the board, you need to:

   a speak to Marek Harlos in production planning (2 hours).
   b prepare drawings of the prototype (4 hours).
   c review the project schedule (3 hours).

   You can plan to do these things whenever you like. Write them in your schedule.

2 You also need to meet with your partner to rehearse your presentation. This will take at least 2 hours. Your partner will call you to schedule a time. Make sure they will have done these things before you meet.

   a updated the budget with new cost estimates
   b run some final prototype tests
   c spoken to the head of R&D
   d prepared your PowerPoint presentation

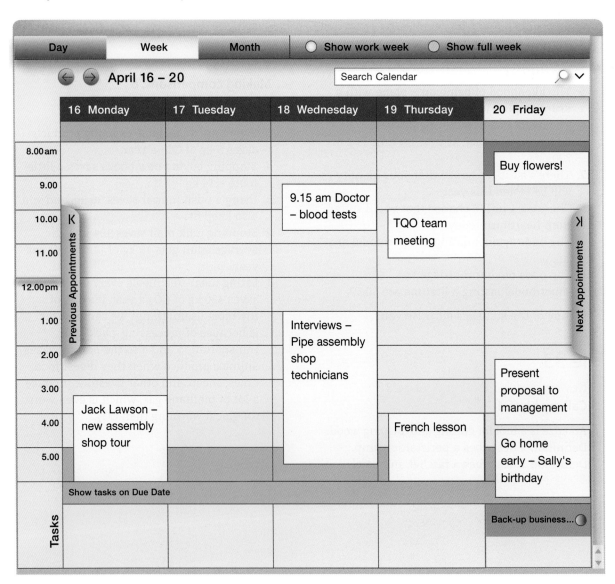

File 37

Unit 18, page 85
Discussing risks, 7

Exercise 6 Answer: You should switch to the other door. It doubles the odds of winning. The probability that you chose a door with the car behind it first time is only one in three. It's more likely you chose a door with a goat.

That means if you switch, you have a two in three chance of winning.

File 38

Unit 3, page 13
Giving instructions, 6

B
These instructions are in the wrong order. Number them in the correct order. Then explain them to your partner. Try to use some of these expressions.

Before you begin ...	First ...	Then ...
Next ...	After that ...	When ...
Once ...		

Changing a toner cartridge
a .... Close the cover and switch the printer on.
b .... Insert a new cartridge.
c .... Open the front cover.
d .... Remove the old toner cartridge.
e .... Switch the printer off.

File 39

Unit 2, page 9
Specifications, 9

The statistics belong to an Indian Elephant.

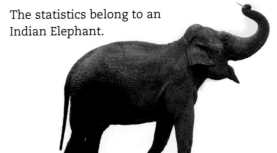

File 40

Unit 5, page 25
Tracking, 6

1
a There is a large number of devices.
b There are more devices than are necessary.
2
a We have as many satellites as we need.
b We have more than two satellites but not very many.
3
a Turn off all the cameras – there are three or more cameras.
b Turn off both the cameras – there are two cameras.
4
a Neither of the speed cameras work – there are two cameras.
b None of the speed cameras work – there are three or more cameras.
5
a There's a short time, but enough to eat and relax.
b There's little time to eat and relax – we need more time.

File 41

Review and Remember 6, page 87
Call my bluff, 2

Here is the correct definition of the word *monocle*. Work together and write two false definitions. Read all three definitions to the class and see if they can guess which definition is correct.

A monocle is a circular lens with a metal ring around the edge. It's attached to a string or chain and people wear it over one eye. The other end of the string or chain is attached to clothing so that if it falls, it can't get broken or lost.

File 42

Review and Remember 2, page 31

Carbon footprint, 2

Answers

1 Lowering the temperature setting of your water heater saves 217 kg of CO_2, but insulation is even better. It saves 454 kg.

2 Washing clothes in cold water will lower your emissions by 228 kg, but with savings of 635 kg, hanging clothes out to dry is much more effective. Tumble dryers are one of the worst home appliances when it comes to power consumption.

3 The average person could prevent 318 kg of CO_2 from being released into the atmosphere over a year by looking after their refrigerator. And they could prevent a lot more (567 kg), by simply switching things off. But even bigger savings come if they adjust their thermostat by half a degree. If people can stay comfortable by wearing fewer clothes during summer months and putting on more layers in the winter, the average household can save 907 kg CO_2.

4 Trees are attractive, cheap, and they reduce the CO_2 in the air. They provide CO_2 savings of 22,680 kg, which is a lot. It's the same as the savings you'd get if you ate locally grown, unprocessed food once a week, because food often has to travel a long way to get to us.

5 A 10% reduction in rubbish from packaging means a CO_2 saving of 454 kg. That's far higher than changing three light bulbs, which provides a saving of 136 kg. But it's much, much lower than double glazed windows which would save 2,536 kg.

File 43

Unit 12, page 57

Describing damage, 8

B

You've been looking after **A**'s home while they're on holiday. Unfortunately some things have gone wrong and you've had a few accidents. Call **A**, and tell them about some things that have been damaged. Use the picture below.

Irregular verbs

Present	Past	Past Participle	Present	Past	Past Participle
be	was / were	been	lie	lay	lain
become	became	become	lose	lost	lost
begin	began	begun	make	made	made
break	broke	broken	mean	meant	meant
bring	brought	brought	meet	met	met
build	built	built	pay	paid	paid
buy	bought	bought	put	put	put
catch	caught	caught	quit	quit	quit
choose	chose	chosen	read	read	read
come	came	come	ride	rode	ridden
cost	cost	cost	ring	rang	rung
cut	cut	cut	rise	rose	risen
deal	dealt	dealt	run	ran	run
do	did	done	saw	sawed	sawn
draw	drew	drawn	say	said	said
drink	drank	drunk	see	saw	seen
drive	drove	driven	sell	sold	sold
eat	ate	eaten	send	sent	sent
fall	fell	fallen	set	set	set
feed	fed	fed	shake	shook	shaken
feel	felt	felt	shoot	shot	shot
find	found	found	show	showed	shown
fly	flew	flown	shut	shut	shut
forbid	forbade	forbidden	sit	sat	sat
forget	forgot	forgotten	sleep	slept	slept
freeze	froze	frozen	speak	spoke	spoken
get	got	got (gotten AmE)	spend	spent	spent
			split	split	split
give	gave	given	spread	spread	spread
go	went	gone	stand	stood	stood
grow	grew	grown	steal	stole	stolen
hang	hung	hung	stick	stuck	stuck
have	had	had	take	took	taken
hear	heard	heard	teach	taught	taught
hide	hid	hidden	tear	tore	torn
hit	hit	hit	tell	told	told
hold	held	held	think	thought	thought
hurt	hurt	hurt	throw	threw	thrown
keep	kept	kept	understand	understood	understood
know	knew	known	wear	wore	worn
lay	lay	laid	write	wrote	written
lead	led	led			
learn	learnt	learnt			
leave	left	left			
lend	lent	lent			
let	let	let			

Numbers

Large numbers

In English we generally use commas to separate the figures in long numbers:

1,000,000,000 = *a/one billion*
1,000,000,000,000 = *a/one trillion*

In American English, you can pronounce round numbers like 1,800 and 2,100 in two ways:

One thousand eight hundred **or** *Eighteen hundred*
Two thousand one hundred **or** *Twenty-one hundred*

This is becoming common in British English, too.

Long numbers

In telephone numbers and other long numbers like account numbers or credit card numbers, we pronounce the figures individually, and grouped in threes or fours:

215 577 9025 = *Two one five, five seven seven, nine oh two five*

In British English you can say *double* to repeat a number:

622 = *six* *double* *two*

In American English, pronounce the numbers separately:

622 = *six, two, two*

Short numbers

Numbers ending –*teen* and –*ty* are easy to confuse. Notice how the stress changes

| 15, 50 | *fifteen, fifty* | oO, Oo |
| 18, 80 | *eighteen, eighty* | oO, Oo |

In British English we generally say *and* before tens in large numbers. This should be left out in American English:

365   *Three hundred **and** sixty-five*
        Three hundred sixty-five

Fractions

$1/4$ = a quarter, $1/3$ = a third, $1/2$ = a half,
$2/3$ = two-thirds $3/4$ = three-quarters,
$7/8$ = seven-eighths

Decimals

In English, a point is used to indicate decimal fractions (not a comma). Numbers are pronounced individually after the point.

14.562 = *fourteen point five six two*
0 is pronounced *zero* or *nought* before the point and *oh* or *zero* after the point

0.6 = *nought point six*
1.04 = *one point oh four*

Money

Money signs are generally written before numbers, but pronounced after.

€50 = *fifty euros*
$900 = *nine hundred dollars*

Dates

In British English we say *the* and *of* but we do not write them:

26th May 2009 = **the** twenty-sixth **of** May, two thousand and nine

In American English, dates are written with the month first:

06/07/2009 = *June (the) seventh, two thousand (and) nine*

Times

Use *a.m.* or *p.m.* to specify before or after noon:

6.45 *a.m.* (before noon)   6.45 *p.m.* (after noon)

In the UK the 24-hour clock is used for plane and train timetables, and often for meetings and other events.

The train leaves at thirteen forty-five (13.45)
In the US it is uncommon.

The train leaves at one forty-five (1.45 p.m.)

Conversions

Length

Imperial to metric		Metric to imperial	
1 inch (in) (")	25.4 millimetres	1 millimetre (mm)	0.039 inches
1 foot (ft) (')	30.48 centimetres	1 centimetre (cm)	0.394 inches
1 yard (y)	91.44 centimetres	1 metre (m)	39.37 inches
1 mile	1,609 metres	1 kilometre (km)	0.621 miles

12 inches = 1 foot   3 feet = 1 yard   1,760 yards = 1 mile

Weight

Imperial to metric		Metric to imperial	
1 ounce (oz)	28.34 grams	1 gram (gm)	0.035 ounces
1 pound (lb)	453.6 grams	1 kilogram (kg)	2.204 pounds
1 stone (s)	6.35 kilograms	1 tonne (t)	1.102 US tons

16 ounces = 1 pound   14 pounds = 1 stone
US weights: 100 pounds = 1 hundredweight (cwt)   20 hundredweight = 1 ton
Old UK weights: 112 pounds = 1 hundredweight (cwt)   20 hundred weight = 1 ton

Speed

1 mile per hour (mph) = 1.6 kilometres per hour (km/h)
1 kilometre per hour (km/h) = 0.621 miles per hour (mph)

Temperature

Volume

Imperial to metric		Metric to imperial	
1 pint (UK)	0.57 litres	1 cc	0.002 pints (US)
1 pint (US)	0.47 litres	1 litre	2.11 pints (US)
1 gallon (UK)	4.546 litres	1 cubic metre	264 gallons (US)
1 gallon (US)	3.785 litres		

Area

Imperial to metric		Metric to imperial	
1 square foot	929 cm^2	1 cm^2	0.155 square inches
1 square yard	0.836 m^2	1 m^2	10.76 square feet
1 acre	4,046.86 m^2	1 km^2	0.386 square miles

To convert Celsius to Fahrenheit: multiply by 9, divide by 5 and add 32.
To convert Fahrenheit to Celsius: subtract 32, multiply by 5 and divide by 9.

Power

To convert horsepower to kilowatts: multiply horsepower by 0.745.
To convert kilowatts to horsepower: multiply kilowatts by 1.341.

British and American English

British English	American English	British English	American English
aerial	antenna	off (It has gone off.)	bad / spoiled (It's gone bad / spoiled.)
aeroplane	airplane		
aluminium	aluminum	motorway	freeway
anticlockwise	counterclockwise	mum	mom
articulated lorry	tractor trailer / trailer truck	parcel	package
		pavement	sidewalk
autumn	fall	pay rise	raise
bank holiday	national holiday	petrol	gas / gasoline
bill (in a restaurant)	check	petrol station	gas station
bin / dustbin	trash can	phone box	telephone booth
bonnet (on a car)	hood	plasterboard	sheetrock
boot (on a car)	trunk	plaster	band-aid
cash dispenser / cashpoint	ATM (automatic teller machine)	pollyfilla	spackle
		polythene	plastic sheeting
cheque	check	postcode	zip code
cooker	range / stove	property	real estate
CV (curriculum vitae)	résumé	rawl plug	anchor
diary	calendar	queue	line
diversion	detour	return (ticket)	round trip ticket
drawing pins	pushpins / thumbtacks	roundabout	traffic circle
		rubber	eraser
estate car	station wagon	run the bath	fill the tub
exhaust pipe (on a car)	tailpipe / muffler	(shopping) trolley	(shopping) cart
extension lead	power strip	skip	dumpster
fire engine	fire truck	spanner	(monkey) wrench
flat battery	dead battery	tap	faucet
football	soccer	timber (wood)	lumber
garden	backyard / yard	toilet / loo / WC	bathroom / restroom
gear stick	stick shift	torch	flashlight
ground floor	first floor	turn left / right	make a left / right
handbag	purse	tyre	tire
holiday	vacation	underground / tube	subway
lead	power cord	university	school
letter box	mailbox	VAT (value added tax)	sales tax
lift	elevator	wardrobe / cupboard	closet
lorry	truck	windscreen	windshield
maths	math		
mobile phone	cell phone		

Listening script

1.1 🎧₂

A   OK, I think we're all here now, so welcome everyone. I'm Larina Rios. I'm responsible for group security, and I'm running today's online class. But before I begin, I'd like to hear from all of you. So please introduce yourselves and tell us a little about the work you do at PTT. George, perhaps you'd like to start? George?

B   Hello, can you hear me?

A   Yes, George – go ahead.

B   Well, my name's George Paterson and I work in the London office. I'm Australian, but I've been living in the UK for about three years now.

A   How long have you been with PTT, George?

B   A month. I work in facility management. We're building a new warehouse in South London and that's what I'm working on right now. Erm …

A   That's great George, thanks. Let's move on to April in China. Hello, April.

C   Hello, everyone. My name's April Wei, and I work in the Shanghai office. I've been with the company for two weeks. I work on the help desk here and we provide technical support to the Asia Pacific Region.

A   What languages do you speak, April?

C   In our group we speak Korean, Japanese, and Mandarin.

A   Excellent. OK, and now India and Amar. Amar, what do you do for us?

D   Good morning, everyone. I'm a website designer and I'm based in Bangalore. I started working at PTT yesterday.

A   Just yesterday? Well congratulations, Amar. How are you getting on with your new job?

D   Very well, thank you. I'm settling into the office here very well.

A   Good. And finally, Joey … Joey, are you there?

E   Hi. I'm Joey Marino and I've been at PTT for two weeks. I'm in charge of a new IT project. Sorry, but I can't go into details because it's top secret.

A   OK, thanks, Joey. We don't want to know. Confidentiality is one of the topics for today's class and we'll talk more about it later. But let's begin by looking at the issue of laptop security. Now you've all received a laptop …

2.1 🎧₃

1   It looks exciting. How fast can it go?
2   Is it built to last? What's it made of?
3   OK, give me the bad news. How much is this going to cost me?
4   I don't like red. What other colours does it come in?
5   What's the maximum payload? Can it carry someone who is really heavy?
6   Does it run on electricity or is it petrol driven?
7   What kind of engine has it got? Is it like the one in my lawn mower?
8   How long will I be able to I ride it before it runs out of petrol?
9   Tell me about the boxes it comes in. How big will they be?
10 When I hit the brakes, how far does it go before it comes to a standstill?

2.2 🎧₄

It's around 640 cm long and about 3.4 metres high, and its top speed is forty kilometres an hour. Its maximum load is around a tonne, and it weighs approximately four and a half tonnes. The colour is grey, and its exterior coating material is leather – a waterproof leather. Its fuel source is bamboo, bananas, and peanuts. Greenhouse gas emissions include CO_2 and methane. And finally, memory – its memory is 100% perfect. It never forgets anything.

2.3 🎧₅

A   So this is the bike? Cool!

B   Yes! It weighs approximately 11 kilograms.

A   So it's easy to lift and move around?

B   Yes, and it has a spring-loaded mechanism in the rear, which allows the rear wheels to move inwards and outwards.

A   So what does that mean?

B   The rear wheels move closer together when the bike goes faster. They separate at low speeds or when the bike isn't moving.

A   Yes, but why?

B   Why?

A   Yes. Why is that helpful?
B   Oh, I see. Well, it's more stable than other bikes.
A   It's less likely to fall over?
B   That's right. Learning to ride a bike can be scary, but with this bike it's not.
A   That's great.
B   And there's another important feature here. The chain's completely covered. See?
A   And the benefit of that is …?
B   It's safer.
A   So you don't have to worry about clothing getting caught up in it.
B   Exactly.
A   I like it!

3.1 🎧 ⑥

1   First, fill the tank with water. Distilled water's best, but it's not essential. Next, switch the machine on and wait a few minutes. When the water's hot enough, the light comes on. After that, you just have to hold the machine against the wall. You'll see the wallpaper darken as it gets wet and then you can start to scrape. The plate gets very hot, so be careful not to touch it or you'll burn yourself. It's best to work downwards and to work on one strip at a time.

2   Before you begin, get some wooden stakes and string, and mark out the area. Make sure you keep the corners square or else you could hit problems when you come to lay the slabs. Once you've marked it out, you need to excavate to a depth of about 12 cm: that's 8 cm for the gravel and 4 cm for the concrete slabs or paving stones. It's important to slope downwards away from the house, otherwise the rainwater won't drain off. Aim for a slope of about 5 mm for every metre. Then you can start laying the gravel.

3   First of all, make sure the subject is sitting or lying down in a comfortable position. Tell them to close their eyes, take a deep breath, and let it out very slowly. Once they've started to relax, tell them to think about their arms. Be careful not to speak too fast, or else it won't work. Tell them to make all their arm muscles loose and limp. It's important to talk with a relaxed and soothing voice, and say lots of positive things like 'That's right, good, you're doing just fine', otherwise they won't have confidence in you. Then, after you've talked about their arms, move on to their legs and tell them to relax all the muscles in their legs. After that move on to other parts of their body speaking with a relaxed …

4.1 🎧 ⑦

1   I left my car outside in a rainstorm and it wouldn't start. I tried turning the key in the ignition, but it was so wet nothing happened. Luckily I had a can of Mr Fixit. I sprayed it all over the wiring around the distributor and tried again. The car started first time. Now I use it on my car locks as well and it stops them freezing in cold weather.

2   Our filing cabinets came from a different office, and they had sticky labels all over them. We tried peeling them, but they were so firmly stuck, we couldn't and they left a residue. Then we thought of Mr Fixit. We sprayed it on and left it to soak. Five minutes later, the labels and the residue came right off.

3   I was fixing up an old bike and I wanted to raise the seat, but it was stuck. I pulled and twisted it, but it was so rusty, it wouldn't budge. I tried putting cooking oil and grease on it, but that didn't work. Then I found a can of Mr Fixit and sprayed it on the seat post. I gave it one tug and the seat came out!

4   In the summer, our bedroom gets too hot to sleep in, so we were very glad when my father gave us an old fan he didn't need. It kept us cool, but it made so much noise we couldn't sleep. My husband squirted the moving parts with Mr Fixit and that did the trick. It doesn't keep us awake anymore.

5.1 🎧 ⑧

1   A   Jack Cabane.
    B   Ah, hello Mr Cabane. Ulla Svensson here.
    A   Hi, Ulla, how are you doing?
    B   The traffic's been a bit heavy, so I'm afraid I won't get to you by ten.
    A   That's OK. Are you on I-95?
    B   Yes, I'm just passing Girard Avenue.
    A   Then you should be here in about twenty minutes. Take the airport exit and follow the signs to the Penn Industrial Park. You'll see our company sign.
    B   OK.
    A   Then call me when you're at the security gate and I'll come and get you.
    B   OK. I'll call again when I'm at the gate.
    A   Excellent. Looking forward to meeting you.
    B   And you. See you in a bit.

2   A   Hello, you must be Ulla. Nice to meet you. I'm Jack.
    B   Nice to meet you too, Jack.
    A   Did you have any trouble finding us?

B No, not at all. The car I rented has a GPS.
A Ah, yes, they're wonderful. Now we need to go to the security desk and get you a badge. Are these your boxes?
B Yes, I brought a few samples for you to look at.
A Great. Then let's sign you in and we can go to my office. Do you need a hand?
B No, I can manage, thanks.
A OK. Is this your first visit to Philadelphia?
B Yes, but I've been to New York a couple of times.

3 B So I'll send you an estimate for the installation when you send us the plans.
A Thanks, I'd appreciate it. And could you send an estimate for maintenance, too?
B Yes, of course. No problem.
A Great. So is that everything?
B Yes, I think so.
A Well, it's been a very useful day.
B Yes, really good. Thank you so much for organizing everything, Jack.
A You're welcome. Just let me know if you need any more information.
B I will. Erm … now how do I get back to my car from here?
A I'll take you there.
B That's very kind of you.
A No problem.

4 A Now would you like me to give you directions back to I-95?
B No, I've got the GPS.
A Oh, of course. OK, well it was great meeting you, Ulla.
B And you.
A We'll be in touch, and have a good flight back to Stockholm.
B Thanks. And thanks once again for all your help today.
A It was a pleasure. Hey, take care.
B Bye, Jack.

6.1 🎧⁹

A Is the site prepared and ready for the installation?
B Yes, it should be. The customer's getting it ready.
A If it's not, it'll be a big problem.
B They've received all the instructions they need.
A What about the electricity supply? We need 240 volts.
B Don't worry. The customer knows about that.
A Is it already installed?
B I don't know. But if it's not there, the customer will install it.

A Do they know about the platform?
B The platform?
A Yes – how strong it needs to be.
B That's not a problem. If the platform isn't strong enough, we'll strengthen it.
A But will we have the tools we need to do that?
B Yes, everything's being delivered.
A But what if something's missing?
B We'll get it couriered over.
A But what if that takes too long?
B Then we'll improvise. Relax, everything's going to be fine.

6.2 🎧¹⁰

A How are you getting to the airport tomorrow?
B My wife will drive me there unless she's busy.
A But what if she's busy?
B Then I'll take the train.
A OK. I'll meet you at the airport at ten, then.
B At ten? But our flight doesn't leave until one.
A I like to get there early in case there are queues at security.
B Isn't two hours enough?
A No, I need to have lunch at the airport. I can't fly unless I've eaten first.
B They'll feed us on the plane.
A Yes, but I'd rather eat first in case I don't like the airline food.

7.1 🎧¹¹

A May I take one of these maps?
B They're 15 euros.
A Oh.
B Yes, they're not free, I'm afraid, but there's a small map in the folder I gave you.
A Then I'll use that. Erm … now what are the speed limits here?
B In France?
A Yes, I've never driven here before.
B Well, on a motorway it's 130 kilometres an hour. But if it's wet, you mustn't drive faster than 110 kilometres an hour, and on a dual carriageway you're allowed to drive at 110 when it's dry …
A Hold on. I must write all this down. Erm … I can't drive faster than 110 kilometres an hour if it's raining …
B Er, it's all in the folder.
A Err … OK.
B But you should be aware. You're not allowed to drive above the speed limit. If the police catch you doing more than 25 kilometres

above it, they can confiscate your licence on the spot.

A So speeding's a serious offence?

B Oh, yes.

A Now, I have to take the car to Spain for a few days. Is that OK?

B Yes.

A I don't have to take out extra insurance cover?

B No. As long as you stay in the EU, it's OK.

A Ah, so I don't need to worry about that.

B No, insurance isn't necessary.

A Now, what time have I got to return the car on Friday?

B By six thirty. Otherwise we have to charge you for an extra day.

A I see.

B And you should try to return it with a full tank of petrol if you can. It's cheaper that way.

A OK. Erm … now one of my colleagues told me that I shouldn't drink and drive here. It's strictly forbidden.

B Well, naturally, you ought to be responsible. But you can probably enjoy one glass of wine. The alcohol limit is point five milligrams per millilitre.

A Zero point five.

B Yes.

A OK!

8.1 ⓬

Hey Chris, what are you doing? Be careful! Chris! Are you OK?
Margaret! Chris is unconscious! Ring for an ambulance. Quick!

8.2 ⓭

2 Back a bit. Back a bit more. Perfect! OK. Hold it there! That's beautiful! Yes. Lovely.

9.1 ⓯

1 A Here it is.

B It's an alarm clock.

A Yes, but it's not just any alarm clock. Look, let me set it and I'll show you how it works. It has a built-in motion detector.

B Oh, what does that mean?

A If you wave your hand in front of it, the alarm will stop ringing.

B You don't have to push a button to make it stop?

A No.

B Cool!

A OK, wave your hand in front of it. Go on.

A See?

B Fantastic.

2 A What are you working on at the moment?

B It's a system for detecting drowsiness when you're driving.

A It looks like a pair of glasses.

B Yes, you wear these glasses when you're driving, and they can measure how drowsy or sleepy you are.

A How do they work?

B They have built-in sensors. They monitor your eyelid movements and other signs of physical tiredness.

A And what'll happen if you get sleepy?

B An alarm'll go off and a loud voice will tell you to wake up.

A Ah. That's very useful.

B It is. If you ask drivers 'Have you ever fallen asleep at the wheel?' nearly half will say 'yes'.

A That's scary.

B Exactly.

3 A I have a question.

B What's that?

A If somebody stole my cash card and used it to withdraw money from a cash machine, who would be responsible? Me or the bank?

B The bank would pay, I think. Unless you gave the thieves your PIN number.

A OK. Suppose the thieves had a gun and they forced me to give them my PIN number.

B Then I'm not sure. But I think the bank would still pay.

A It must cost banks a lot of money.

B Yeah.

A Then we should invent a cash card with two PIN numbers – one number for normal use and the other for emergencies. If you typed in the emergency number, it'd call the police.

B But if you called the police, the thieves might get angry or violent.

A If the cash machine delivered the money, how would they know? They'd think everything was OK.

B Yes, I see. That might work.

4 B What's this? Another one of your crazy inventions?

A This one isn't crazy. It's really useful.

B It looks like a cigarette.

A It's a self-extinguishing cigarette.

B You're kidding.

A No, don't laugh. Burning cigarettes start a lot of house fires.

B OK. How does it work?

A Well, this cigarette has a little bag of water in the filter at the end, and also a detonator. See?

B Mmm. So if it burns down to the filter, the detonator will explode.

A That's right. And that'll burst the bag of water and put the cigarette out.

B Before it starts a fire and burns the house down.

A Exactly!

B Mmm. How much would they cost to manufacture?

A If my calculations are correct, about twice as much as normal cigarettes.

B Twice as much! Everyone would give up smoking.

A Yes. That's another reason it's a good idea.

5 A Slow down, there's a speed bump.

B I hate those things.

A Me, too.

B Someone should invent intelligent speed bumps.

A How would they work?

B Well, you could make them out of smart polymer materials that could measure speed. If you drove over them too fast, er … they'd expand.

A And give you a big bump.

B And if you were going slowly you could drive over them smoothly.

A Mmm. Would that work?

B It's possible in theory, but I don't know if it'd work in practice.

A They might cost too much to produce.

B Yeah.

A Nice idea though.

10.1 ⒃

1 A I heard George Wilson was in hospital … George Wilson?

B Yes.

A I thought he worked on your team?

B He does.

A I heard he had an operation on his knee … is that right?

B Yes, that's right.

A How did it go?

B Fine.

A That's excellent news. I used to work with George in Dubai.

B I see.

A So anyway, what's the weather like in London at the moment?

B It's OK.

A Good, good …

2 A So, where are you from, Angus? England?

B No, I'm from Scotland. Have you ever been there?

A Do you like it here?

B Yes, very much. My wife loves our apartment and our children like their new school.

A Is it cold in England?

B Well, I'm from Scotland – Aberdeen – and yes, it's pretty cold there – much colder than here.

A Are you used to hot weather?

B No, but I'm sure I'll get used to it soon.

A Are you married?

B Erm, yes.

A Do you have any children?

B Well, yes. I have two kids. Hamish is four and Gill is six.

3 A We saw a movie last night – *The Safety Trap*.

B It's a thriller, isn't it?

A That's right. It was really good.

B I don't like thrillers.

A Oh. Have you seen any good films lately?

B No. I had to work on the night shift last month.

A Oh, that's a pity. Still, you're back on the day shift now.

B Yes, I just got used to working nights and they put me back on the day shift.

A That must be difficult for you.

B Yes. They're always changing things around here. I hate it.

A Oh …

10.2 ⒄

A This is a lovely building.

B Thank you. It's brand new. We love it.

A Did you use to have a factory in York Road?

B Yes, that's closed now. We all moved here a few months ago.

A Is the location better for you here?

B Yes, it's more central and we like that. The only downside is the traffic. The roads get busy here in the rush hour.

A Yes, I can imagine. Is parking a problem?

B It's a bit of a nuisance, but we're getting used to it. And this place is twice as big.

A Really? That's amazing.

11.1 ⒅

C What's wrong with it?

D It's really bad. The drive shaft's broken.

A Oh, that's terrible.

B Can we repair it?

D No, there's absolutely nothing we can do about it.

B How much water do we have?

A About eight litres – so about two litres each.

C Well, we've got two alternatives. We can wait here and hope someone finds us, or we can walk.

D I think we should walk. We've got a compass and a map.

C If we continue in this direction, we'll come to a town in thirty kilometres.

A That's too far.

D A car might come along and give us a lift.

B We haven't seen a car all day.

A We'd get tired very quickly walking in this heat.

B Yes, it's too hot. It'd be exhausting.

D It'll cool down tonight.

C That's another problem. It'll get very cold.

D We'll be freezing. It'd be better to keep moving.

A We need to stay with the vehicle.

B When we don't arrive, they'll send a search party to look for us.

C It could take days to find us.

D Why don't we toss a coin? Heads we stay. Tails we walk.

11.2 🎧 19

A First of all, you shouldn't try to walk to the town. You'd never make it.

B Yes, we thought that was a bad idea.

A Good. Now what about the items from the plane?

C We think the large knife is extremely useful.

B We could use it to make a shelter and cut up wood for a fire.

A Exactly. And the cigarette lighter's extremely useful, too.

B But why? It's empty.

A You need to start the fire and you have no matches. You need something to make a spark.

B Oh, I see.

A Keeping warm is going to be your main problem so the space blankets are really useful, too.

C How about the compass?

A That's of little use because you're not going anywhere. The map might be helpful for starting a fire, but only if it's dry.

B What's the aluminium foil for?

A You can use it to make a dry surface to build the fire on. And you can fold it up to make a container to heat snow in. You need to melt snow for water. It's really useful.

C Erm … why do we need to melt snow? We thought we could just eat it.

A You'd need to eat six kilos of snow to consume just half a litre of water. It'd lower your body temperature too much.

C OK, so melt the snow first.

B Next is the cosmetic mirror. Not much use, huh?

A Oh, no, extremely useful. You can signal with it. And you can signal with the gun, too, of course.

B Oh, we thought we'd be starving so we could hunt wild animals for food.

A That'd take too much energy. But the gun's useful as a sound signalling device.

C Can we signal with the sunglasses, too?

A The mirror's better for that, but the sunglasses could protect your face from the wind and prevent snow blindness.

B Now what about the whiskey? That has to be useful for keeping us warm.

A No, you shouldn't drink it. It'd reduce your body temperature and you'd get dehydrated. But you can eat the jelly bean sweets if you get hungry. They don't take much water to digest and they taste nice, too.

12.1 🎧 20

A Hello?

B Err… is that the SoftSolve help desk?

A Yeah, that's right. What do you want?

B I'm having problems trying to install the Project Planner program I downloaded from your site. The activation key doesn't work.

A OK. Give me your order number.

B Sorry?

A I can't sort it out without your order reference number.

B And where would I find that?

A On the invoice we emailed you.

B OK. It's X6 hyphen 79 …

A I don't need the hyphens.

B X6 792 44. … Hello? Hello, are you still there?

A Yes, I'm just looking it up. OK, you're Tomas Vega of Grupo Diaz, right?

B Yes, that's right.

A So, what's the problem then?

B I just said. The activation key you sent doesn't work.

A Are you sure you didn't make a mistake when you typed it in?

B Absolutely sure! I copied and pasted it from the email you sent.

A Then it's your antivirus program that's causing the problem.

B So what do I need to do?

A Switch your antivirus program off and then reinstall. If that doesn't work, call us back.

B But how do I switch it off … ?

12.2 🎧(21)

A Good morning. SoftSolve. Melanie speaking. How can I help?

B Hi. I'm having problems trying to install the Project Planner program I downloaded from your site. The activation key doesn't seem to work.

A I'm sorry to hear that. Can I have the order reference number from the top of the invoice we emailed you and we can sort it out.

B OK. It's X6 hyphen 792 hyphen 44.

A Thanks. I'm just calling the order up on my screen now. Sorry to keep you waiting. It looks like the system's a little slow today. Um ... ah, here it is. So you're Mr Tomas Vega of Grupo Diaz?

B That's right.

A And your activation key appears to be faulty?

B Yes.

A Well, there can sometimes be an issue if you use lower case letters.

B I don't think so. I copied and pasted it from the email you sent.

A Good. Then it sounds as if your antivirus program might be causing the problem.

B So what do I need to do?

A Switch it off and reinstall. I can help you with that now. Are you at your computer?

B Yes.

A Great, then please click on Start ... and then click the program menu. Which antivirus program do you use? ...

B That's great.

A So it's up and running?

B Yes, that's terrific. Thanks a lot.

A You're welcome. And if you need any further assistance, just call us again.

12.3 🎧(22)

1 A What happened to the car?

B Something went wrong with the brakes and Jack ran into a tree. He's OK but the windscreen's broken.

A Looks like the front got dented, too. How did it happen?

B We think it was leaking brake fluid. Jack noticed a light, but he didn't realize it was a warning light.

A Until the brakes failed?

B That's right.

2 A Make sure the technicians use ladders when they're servicing the tank.

B OK.

A Because one of the pipes got bent last time they serviced it.

B Really?

A Yes. We think it got trodden on. And make sure they grease all the joints.

B All right.

A One or two are starting to go rusty.

B Don't worry. I'll tell them.

3 A The water pressure's very low.

B That's strange. Has the hose got twisted or blocked somewhere?

A Maybe.

B Or perhaps the filter's dirty.

A There's a filter?

B Yes, didn't you know?

A No.

B You've got to clean it every now and again because it gets clogged.

A Ah. You didn't tell me that.

13.1 🎧(23)

A So, Emily, you work for PGM.

B That's right.

C That's an engineering company?

B Yes. I've worked there since I left school nine years ago. I started as a mechanic. Then after three years, I changed jobs and became a production planner.

C Have you ever been involved in any environmental or conservation projects before?

B No, this will be my first. But I speak a little Portuguese.

A That's wonderful.

C How come?

B I had a Portuguese boyfriend when I was younger.

C Have you ever been to South America?

B No, but about four years ago I took six months off work and I travelled across the Sahara. I worked for a TV crew.

A How interesting.

B Yes. I'm a qualified mechanic so I was the troubleshooter for any mechanical problems – erm, repairing vehicles, the generators and some of their other equipment.

C But you've never worked on any scientific research projects?

B No, not yet, but I'm willing to work hard and learn. I've got a lot of experience in planning work processes and I'm good at organizing things – events, schedules. I'm good with computers, too.

C But no research experience.

B No.

A I have a different question. The nearest town will be a long way away. How do you feel about that?

C Yes, and living conditions will be rough.

B I've been thinking hard about that recently. I know it won't be easy, but I'm very practical. So I don't think there will be any problems I can't solve. I've wanted to help save the rainforests ever since I saw *An Inconvenient Truth*. I feel very passionate about it.

13.2 (24)

A How's it going?
B Not too good.
A I heard you're behind schedule.
B Yeah.
A This job has to be finished by Friday.
B We're doing our best. All the rain at the weekend didn't help.
A Well, the weather's good today.
B Watch out.
A It's a busy street, isn't it?
B Yeah. The traffic's been a problem. And parked cars, too.
A Have the police put up 'No parking' signs?
B Yes, but nobody reads them. We have to wait while the cars are towed away.
A How far along are you?
B We're laying the cable – we're about half way.
A Only half way? The trenches should be filled in by now.
B We only finished digging them yesterday. That was another problem …
A Why?
B One of the excavators broke a water main.
A Oh, no.
B We've fixed it, but it set us back.
A Well, the deadline can't be extended. This job has to be done by Friday.
B What kind of car do you drive?
A A Renault. Why?
B There's a blue Renault being towed away over there.
A Oh, no! Hey, stop!

14.1 (25)

A Here's the description of the equipment. It's just a first draft.
B I think we can improve it.
A Mmm. Let's cut the word *new* in the first sentence for a start.
B Yes, all innovations are new.
A Exactly. *New* is redundant. Erm … and there's a mistake here. Look. We need a full stop after *night*.

B Yes, and *water* needs a capital letter.
A The word *cooled* is spelt wrongly.
B Yes, it just needs one *l*. OK …
A Oh, look, there's a repeated word.
B Where's that?
A The word *the* – to cool the building the *the* next day.
B Got it. OK.
A Erm … I don't like the last paragraph.
B No, neither do I. We should cut the word *fantastic*.
A I agree. It's not technical.
B And I think *well below* is vague.
A In what way?
B What does *well below* mean?
A Well below the minimum night air temperature?
B That's right, but what exactly does *well below* mean? Can we be more specific? Do we have any figures for this?
A Yes. It cooled the water to 12 degrees Fahrenheit below the minimum night air temperature.
B Then let's say that.
A OK. So the system cooled up to two gallons per square foot of roof surface to 12 degrees Fahrenheit below the minimum night air temperature.
B Good.
A Yes. That's much better.
B Excellent.

14.2 (26)

A Is this gauge suitable?
B Mm. I'm not sure.
A The great thing about it is it's transparent, so you can see the liquid level inside. The end blocks and mounting bolts are aluminium of course, but the central cylinder is nylon.
B What kind of pressure can it withstand?
A 8.5 bar.
B Er, what's that in terms of pounds per square inch?
A One bar is roughly 14.4 PSI.
B So if we multiply it by 14.4 …
A Yes.
B It's somewhere around 120 PSI. OK. What kind of heat can it withstand?
A The maximum operating temperature is 110 degrees Celsius.
B And in Fahrenheit?
A That's a bit more complicated. We need to take the temperature in Celsius, multiply it by nine over five and then add 32.
B So it's 110 times nine, divided by five, plus 32 ….

A   That's right.
B   That's exactly 230 degrees Fahrenheit.
A   Does that sound OK?
B   Yes, that would work. What price can they give us?
A   They're 18.50 a piece.
B   Mmm-hm. And the discount?
A   We could subtract 12% from that for quantities of a hundred or more.
B   So 100 would be 1,850, minus 12% …
A   Yes. So take away 222.
B   OK. That works out to 1,628. And that's dollars?
A   Er, no, euros.
B   Ah!

15.1 🎧⁽²⁷⁾

It was quite a job to trace the main sewer line, but we now know where it runs. We discovered the pipe begins in the south-west corner of the administration building and then runs south-east to the gatehouse. This first part of the pipe is metal. We connected radio transmitters to it, and it was pretty easy to see where it changes direction.

At the gatehouse, it turns south-west, and then west. It runs parallel to the railway track until it gets to a point roughly level with the south-west corner of the assembly shop.

That's where the job got tricky. The metal pipe becomes a concrete pipe at that point, and we had to use acoustic locators. We found the pipe suddenly veers north-east, passing under the canteen and heading towards the lab. But just before it gets there, it veers north-west and goes to the foundry.

Under the foundry, it becomes a metal pipe again, but it's buried very deep in the ground. It was too deep to attach radio transmitters, so we had to place a coil above it and induce a signal.

We discovered it goes south-west from the foundry, goes under the machine shop, and crosses the road to the paint shop. In the middle of the paint shop it changes direction and goes to the assembly shop. But then it does a U-turn and heads north-west again. Just before it reaches the paint shop, it becomes a clay pipe, so the signals disappeared.

We had to insert radio transmitters into the pipe to find out where it goes next. We discovered that it heads directly west. Then just between tank 1 and 2, it turns north and exits the site.

15.2 🎧⁽²⁸⁾

1 A   Hey, Jack.
   B   Yes?
   A   Is that oil or dirt on the floor?
   B   Where?
   A   By the milling machine.
   B   It's just a bit of dirt. I'll clean it up later.
   A   But look, the floor's scratched, too.
   B   Is it?
   A   Yes. It looks like the machine's been vibrating.
   B   You might be right.
   A   You need to ask maintenance to check it out.
   B   OK.
   A   As soon as possible.
   B   OK. I'll see to it.
   A   And someone needs to sweep up. People can't see if the equipment's leaking if the floors are dirty.
   B   OK. I'll take care of it.

2 A   Let's focus on clearing the work area first.
   B   OK.
   A   Do you need these boxes?
   B   No, we can throw them away.
   A   Good. Then stick a red tag on them and put them in the corner for now. We can get rid of them later.
   B   All right.
   A   What about this plastic sheeting?
   B   We'd better hold on to that. We use it all the time.
   A   How about these tools?
   B   They're broken, but I might be able to fix some of them. Do you want me to sort through them?
   A   Yes, but not now.
   B   Perhaps we can recycle them.
   A   Just stick a red tag on them and put them in the corner. Let's get on with clearing the work area. What about these pallets?

3 A   What's this ladder doing in the middle of the store?
   B   I just used it to look for some parts, and I haven't got round to putting it away.
   A   Have you found the parts you need?
   B   Yeah. They were just in the wrong place. I'll tidy up in a minute.
   A   How do people know where things go in this store?
   B   There's a system, but it's a little hard to figure it out.
   A   Then let's come up with a simpler system.
   B   Some of the shelves don't have labels.
   A   Oh, I see.
   B   They keep falling off.

A   Then let's get some labels with stronger adhesive.

B   If they were different colours, we could colour code the parts.

A   Could you organize this place so people can find things more easily?

B   Yes. I'll work something out.

16.1 🎧 29

A   Where are we with the printed circuit boards?

B   If the figures from marketing are correct, we'll need about 2,500 a month.

A   Mmm. Then it's time to find a supplier. We need to give the drawings to John Walker in purchasing.

B   OK, I'll email them to him.

A   Are the drawings ready?

B   We may have to make small changes, but they're good enough to get accurate price estimates.

A   OK. Warn him the design may change a little and ask him to get quotes from three or four suppliers. Let's set up a meeting next week to discuss them.

B   When's a good day for you?

A   Er, Wednesday or Thursday would be best, I think.

B.   Wednesday's the 17th, isn't it?

A   Yes.

B   I'm tied up that day.

A   OK. See if John's free on Thursday.

B   What about samples?

A   Well, if he can get samples, too, that would be great. See if he can manage it by Thursday, but tell him not to worry too much if he can't.

B   OK. Is there anything else?

A   No, I don't think so.

B   I'll email him now, then.

A   Thanks.

17.1 🎧 30

A   I've just spoken with the customer.

B   Did you tell them about the breakdown?

A   Yes, I explained that one of our machines is out of action. They say we can have more time.

B   Ah, good.

A   But if we can't deliver in two weeks, they'll cancel the order.

B   Two weeks?

A   Yes.

B   Ooh. That's going to be difficult. Can they give us three?

A   No. They'll have run out of stock in three weeks. When will the machine be fixed?

B   Next week, maybe.

A   But it broke down a week ago. It's already been out of action for a week.

B   Yes, the maintenance crew have been waiting for a new part.

A   A new part?

B   Yes. A ring had worked loose and it damaged the rotor.

A   So the rotor needs replacing?

B   Yes. It could take a week for the new one to arrive.

A   But the machine will have been out of action for two weeks at that point.

B   I know.

A   I'm going to speak to the maintenance crew. I'll tell them to find another rotor somehow.

B   You can try.

A   We can't wait another week.

B   That's true.

A   And I'm going to tell them this is all their fault.

B   Really?

A   Yes. The machine broke down because it hadn't been serviced properly.

B   Well ...

A   What's the matter?

B   If we want this fixed, we should tell them they've been doing a great job, and we know they can solve this problem.

18.1 🎧 31

A   Have you heard?

B   Heard what?

A   Photos of the new prototype have appeared on the web.

C   Oh, I thought it was supposed to be top secret.

A   It was. The head of security's furious.

B   I don't see how it happened. The doors of the lab are always locked.

C   Who took the photos? Does anyone know?

A   No, but we think they were taken with a mobile phone.

B   Mobile phones aren't allowed in the laboratory.

C   Everyone's supposed to hand in cameras and mobile phones before they go in there.

A   Well, someone didn't. And someone's going to be in deep trouble over this.

B   Well, I always hand in my phone.

C   Yes, me, too.

B   Half a dozen electricians were working in the lab last week – outside contractors.

C   That's right. They were installing some cabling.

A They should have been accompanied by a security guard.

B But they were.

A The whole time?

B Yes, I think so.

A The prototype should have been covered with a sheet if there were outside contractors around. Anyway, I just thought I'd let you know.

C Yeah, thanks.

A The head of security is going to be investigating, of course. Bye now.

B Yeah, bye.

C It's crazy. How is one security guard supposed to watch over six electricians?

B I don't know. But we uncovered the prototype when the contractors were there.

C We couldn't work on it when it was under the sheets.

B I know, but we shouldn't have done that.

C Oh. It's crazy.

B What are we going to tell the head of security?

18.2 🎧 (32)

A Hi. I'm in the busy streets of Bristol today with Dr Ian Walker and oh my, the traffic's bad. Is it always like this, Dr Walker?

B Well, yes, Claire, it usually is.

A Lots of cars and lots of cyclists. Now, Dr Walker, you're a traffic psychologist from the University of Bath, right?

B That's right.

A And you've been researching an important safety issue for cyclists: helmets.

B Yes.

A Could you tell us what you've discovered?

B Yes, Claire. Our most important finding is this: Overtaking vehicles are more likely to come closer if you are wearing a helmet.

A How did you discover this?

B We fitted my bike with an ultrasonic distance sensor and I recorded about two thousand three hundred motorists overtaking me.

A How close did the motorists come?

B It varied. But if I wore a helmet, they came closer. Twenty-five percent more vehicles passed within one metre of my bike when I was wearing a helmet.

A And that's a big problem?

B Yes, because cyclists need room to deal with obstacles in the road.

A So cyclists are more likely to be knocked down if they wear a helmet?

B Err, no. I don't know if that's true or not. Seventy-five per cent of accidents with cars and bikes happen at junctions. I didn't study those. I just studied what happens when motorists are overtaking.

A OK. Now, you did another experiment with a wig, didn't you?

B Yes. I put on a long wig so it looked like I had long hair. I wanted to know if it makes a difference if drivers think they're overtaking a female cyclist.

A And does it?

B Yes. If motorists think you're female, the chances are they'll give you more room.

A So should cyclists throw away their helmets and start wearing wigs instead?

B Well, it's not that simple. Helmets are useful in low-speed falls – so they're very good for children. We're just not sure about accidents with cars. People disagree about whether they reduce the risk of head injury.

A But you had two accidents when you were doing the experiment?

B Yes, I was hit by a bus and a truck.

A Oh, my!

B Both times I was wearing my helmet, but I didn't hit my head.

A Do you always wear a helmet now?

B No, I tend not to.

A And what are the odds of you being knocked off your bike on your way home today?

B Oh, there's no chance of that. I came by car.

A Dr Walker, thank you very much and have a safe journey home.

B Thanks, Claire.

OXFORD
UNIVERSITY PRESS

Great Clarendon Street, Oxford OX2 6DP

Oxford University Press is a department of the University of Oxford.
It furthers the University's objective of excellence in research, scholarship,
and education by publishing worldwide in

Oxford New York

Auckland Cape Town Dar es Salaam Hong Kong Karachi
Kuala Lumpur Madrid Melbourne Mexico City Nairobi
New Delhi Shanghai Taipei Toronto

With offices in

Argentina Austria Brazil Chile Czech Republic France Greece
Guatemala Hungary Italy Japan Poland Portugal Singapore
South Korea Switzerland Thailand Turkey Ukraine Vietnam

OXFORD and OXFORD ENGLISH are registered trade marks of
Oxford University Press in the UK and in certain other countries

© Oxford University Press 2009

The moral rights of the authors have been asserted.

Database right Oxford University Press (maker)

First published 2009
2020 2019
15 14 13 12

ISBN: 978 0 19 457541 6

Printed in China

ACKNOWLEDGEMENTS

*The authors and publisher are grateful to those who have given permission to reproduce
the following extracts and adaptations of copyright material:* pp101, 104 Quiz content
source: www.kyero.com, Spanish Property Portal. Reproduced by permission.
p50 Quotations reproduced by permission of the individuals: Terry Sejnowski,
Bruce Lahn, Nathan Myhrvold, Chris McKay, and Elizabeth Loftus. p80 'Product
recall notice' from www.tradingstandards.gov.uk. Reproduced by permission
of the Trading Standards Institute. p83 from 'Social Engineering Fundamentals
– A True Story' by Sarah Granger, 18 December 2001 from www.securityfocus.
com. Reproduced by permission of the author and Security Focus. p119
Fictional Interview with Dr Ian Walker. Reproduced by kind permission
of Dr Ian Walker.

Text sources: p46 www.blog.khymos.org; p64 www.builditsolar.com; pp10, 84,
88, 94, 100 Time Magazine reviews of best inventions (2005 and 2006); pp70,
97 www.lamar.colostate.edu; p84 Life: the Odds, by Gregory Baer, pub. Gotham
Books, division of Penguin Books, USA. First printing October 2003; p92
chindogu.com

Illustrations by: Peter Bull Art Studio pp13, 36, 40, 46, 47, 67, 76, 80, 88 (jobs),
89, 90 (spanner), 92 (bed), 94 (toothbrush), 96 (socket); Martin Cottam p66;
Cyrus Deboo pp23, 28, 56, 73, 77; Mark Duffin pp18 (Mr Fixit), 20, 24, 88
(magic door); Tim Kahane p45; Bill Ledger pp14, 15, 49, 51 (robot), 85; Annabel
Milne pp9, 53, 87, 90 (andiron), 92 (crook), 94 (flail), 96 (drill chuck), 98, 100,
103; Ben Morris pp17, 32, 37, 57, 64, 70, 104; Sarah Nicholson pp5, 29, 51
(diagram), 62, 69, 79, 95, 99, 102, 107; Garry Parsons pp18 (people needing
help), 34, 39, 54, 63, 72, 93, 97

*The publisher would like to thank the following for their kind permission to reproduce
photographs and other copyright material:* Alamy pp12 (hypnotist/Bubbles
Photolibrary), 27 (Gobi Desert/Peter Adams Photography), 28 (vapour trails/
Imagebroker), 30 (diamond ring/Woodystock, Steel bars/Imagebroker, car
manufacturing/Chad Ehlers, coffee beans/David R Frazier Photolibrary. Inc,
cup of coffee/Cephas Picture Library), 33 (security/Nordicphotos, departure
lounge/PCL, on board/Wild Places Photography, customs/David Pearson), 42
(mp3 player/Woodystock, toothbrush/Joe Tree, memory stick/StockImages,
TV remote/Picturesbyrob, GPS system/INSADCO Photography), 48 (canteen/
INSADCO Photography), 60 (straw house/Jeff Morgan Alternative Technology,
carer/Enigma), 64 (sprinkler/Rob Walls), 75 (circuit board/Andrew Paterson),
78 (electro engine/Picture Contact), 82 (scientists/Moodboard); Arbortech
pp8, 90 (Airboard); Corbis pp12 (laying patio/construction photography),
16 (unexploded firework/Sygma/Touhig Sion), 33 (immigration/David Brabyn),
35 (eye dropper, hay fever relief/Everett Kennedy Brown/epa), 42 (Post-it note/
Lew Robertson), 52 (Desert/Gavin Hellier/JAI); Digital Vision p31 (tree planting/
Peter Dazeley); Dorling Kindersley pp12 (wallpaper stripper/Gary Ombler),
42 (lawnmower/Peter Andersen); Dutchtub.com p9 (Dutchtub); Getty Images
pp7 (woman on computer/Paul Bradbury, men eating pizza/Jacobs Stock
Photography), 31 (washing/Mark Lewis) 38 (photocopier/Iconica/ColorBlind
Images), 84 (cyclist/Robert House/Uppercut Images), 94 (interview/David Lees),
103 (elephant/Dave King), 104 (switch/Jeffrey Hamilton, washing machine/Roy
Mehta); Groovy Movie Picture House pp21 (solar cinema); Jupiter Images p85
(tossing coin/Image Source); Harper Collins, the International Chindogu
Society, and Dan Papia p92 (tie, umbrella, T-shirt, baby clothes); The Kobal
Collection pp20 (ET/Universal); Morphy Richards p42 (electric blanket); Ted
Morrison pp40 (shrinking fabric), 41 (optical fibres in concrete/egg impacting
silicone); nemoequipment.com p11 (Hypno PQ tent); Olisio p100 (iron); OUP
pp4 (woman wearing headset), 11 (firework), 33 (airport check-in), 40 (fabric),
78 (electric wires); projectcartoon.com p86 (project reviews); Punchstock p75
(woman on mobile); Science Photo Library p30 (raw diamonds/Ted Kinsman),
83 (access denied/Laguna Design); Scott Shim, Matt Grossman, Ryan Lightbody
p10 (Shift bike); Seitz Phototechnic AG (www.roundshot.ch) p9 (panoramic
camera); John Sydes p62 (road works); Vestergaard Frandsen Inc p10 (LifeStraw).

Cover image by: F. Schussler/PhotoLink/Photodisc courtesy of OUP Picture Bank

The authors would like to thank many people for their help when writing
this book. Thanks are due to Manfred Heller and Gerlinde Loibl for sharing
their knowledge and expertise on global warming and Gerhard Schöllhammer
for help with a variety of technical questions. We'd also like to thank Evdoxia
Tsakiridou and Christopher Frank for their help in identifying interesting
products, ideas, and processes for the book. Our thanks also go to students
at BMW AG, EADS Deutschland GmbH and Harrison Clinical Research
Deutschland GmbH for letting us trial materials in their classes. Many
thanks, too, to our colleagues Robert Hilliard and Joseph Zimmerman for
their helpful thoughts and comments on the materials. Similar thanks
extend to the readers and trialers who include: Bill Cheesman, OISE, Oxford,
UK; Dita Galova, Faculty of Mechanical Engineering, Brno University of
Technology; Chris Cote, Infolangues; Christa Laederach; Andrew McLarty;
Joëlle Paulin, CCI Saone et Loire. We'd also like to thank our editor, Lewis
Lansford, for his help, support, and constructive comments on our
manuscript. Last but not least, we'd like to thank our spouses for their
patience, tolerance, and good humour while we worked on the manuscript.